STRATEGIC
INTELLIGENCE

STRATEGIC INTELLIGENCE

*Business Intelligence, Competitive
Intelligence, and Knowledge Management*

Jay Liebowitz

Auerbach Publications
Taylor & Francis Group
Boca Raton   New York

Auerbach Publications is an imprint of the
Taylor & Francis Group, an informa business

Published in 2006 by
Auerbach Publications
Taylor & Francis Group
6000 Broken Sound Parkway NW, Suite 300
Boca Raton, FL 33487-2742

International Standard Book Number-10: 0-8493-9868-1 (Hardcover)
International Standard Book Number-13: 978-0-8493-9868-1 (Hardcover)
Library of Congress Card Number 2005057213

Library of Congress Cataloging-in-Publication Data

Liebowitz, Jay, 1957-
  Strategic intelligence : business intelligence, competitive intelligence, and knowledge management / Jay Liebowitz
        p. cm.
  Includes bibliographical references and index.
  ISBN 0-8493-9868-1 (alk. paper)
  1. Business intelligence--Management. 2. Knowledge management. 3. Strategic planning. 4. Business intelligence--Case studies. I. Title.

HD38.7.L54 2006
658.4'72--dc22   2005057213

Visit the Taylor & Francis Web site at
http://www.taylorandfrancis.com

and the Auerbach Publications Web site at
http://www.auerbach-publications.com

Dedication

To those practitioners, educators, and organizations
who are leading the way in bringing closer together
as a family the knowledge management, business intelligence,
and competitive intelligence communities.

Contents

II: CASE STUDIES

About the Editor

Jay Liebowitz, D.Sc., is a full professor in the Graduate Division of Business and Management at Johns Hopkins University and program director for the Graduate Certificate in Competitive Intelligence at Johns Hopkins University. Prior to joining Johns Hopkins, he was the first knowledge management officer at NASA Goddard Space Flight Center. Before NASA, he served as the Robert W. Deutsch Distinguished Professor of Information Systems at the University of Maryland–Baltimore County, professor of Management Science at George Washington University, and Chaired Professor of Artificial Intelligence (AI) at the U.S. Army War College. He is the founder and editor-in-chief of *Expert Systems with Applications: An International Journal* (published by Elsevier), and the founder and chairperson of The World Congress on Expert Systems. He has published 31 books and a multitude of articles dealing with expert and intelligent systems, knowledge management, and information technology management. His newest books are *Communicating as IT Professionals* (Prentice Hall, 2006) and *Addressing the Human Capital Crisis in the Federal Government: A Knowledge Management Perspective,* published by Butterworth–Heinemann/Elsevier (2004). He also recently completed a study on "Bridging the Knowledge and Skills Gaps: Tapping Federal Retirees" for the IBM Center for the Business of Government. He is a Fulbright Scholar, IEEE-USA Federal Communications Commission Executive Fellow, and Computer Educator of the Year (International Association for Computer Information Systems). He has consulted and lectured worldwide for numerous organizations. He can be reached at 301-315-2893 or at jliebow1@jhu.edu.

Contributors

Thomas E. Kern
Senior Associate
The Annie E. Casey Foundation
Baltimore, Maryland

Maritza Morales
Director of Business Intelligence
Motorola, Inc.
Schaumburg, Illinois

Peter McKenney
CEO/Managing Director
Cipher Systems LLC
Crofton, Maryland

Shereen Remez
Director
Knowledge Management
American Association of Retired Persons
Washington, D.C.

Stephan Berwick
Manager
Business Development/Business
  Intelligence Unit
Northrop Grumman
Herndon, Virginia

Todd Drake
Vice President, Sales
i2, a ChoicePoint Company
Springfield, Virginia

Bill McGilvery
Vice President, Business Development
i2, a ChoicePoint Company
Springfield, Virginia

Liza Puterman
Business Development Associate
i2, a ChoicePoint Company
Springfield, Virginia

Keith B. Johnston
Vice President of Intelligence Programs
The Analysis Corporation
McLean, Virginia

Clint Gauvin
Manager, Intelligence and Law
  Enforcement
The Analysis Corporation
McLean, Virginia

Francisco J. Cantu
Dean of Graduate Research
Tecnológico de Monterrey
Monterrey N.L.
México

Silvia P. Mora
Tecnológico de Monterrey
Monterrey N.L.
México

Aldo Díaz
Tecnológico de Monterrey
Monterrey N.L.
México

Héctor Ceballos
Tecnológico de Monterrey
Monterrey N.L.
México

Sergio O. Martínez
Tecnológico de Monterrey
Monterrey N.L.
México

Daniel R. Jiménez
Tecnológico de Monterrey
Monterrey N.L.
México

Arik Johnson
Founder and CEO of Aurora WDC
Chief Strategist of Aurora's Research and
  Analysis Support Bureau (ReconG2)
Managing Director of Aurora's CI Best
  Practices Institute
Chippewa Falls, Wisconsin

Preface

When I first thought of writing this book, people were asking, "What does strategic intelligence have to do with anything? Is this a book about military intelligence?" Strategic intelligence (SI) has mostly been used in military and defense settings, but its worth goes well beyond that limited role. My view of SI is that every organization should be doing it, as it applies towards improving the strategic decision making process of an entity. That is the thrust of this book.

My experience in the knowledge management (KM), business intelligence (BI), and competitive intelligence (CI) fields has indicated that there are tremendous synergies between these areas. The ultimate goal is how to best use internal and external intelligence for making better decisions. In the same way that knowledge management is being used to break down the silos, so does this need to happen as a whole with the KM, BI, and CI disciplines. Each of these communities seems to be working in isolation; the walls should be demolished to maximize the collective value of what these disciplines offer to the organization.

To help better understand the role of SI in the organization as the KM, BI, and CI fields merge, this book aids the decision maker in applying its underlying concepts. The first part of the book discusses the convergence of KM, BI, and CI into SI. The second part of the book describes case studies written by respected individuals from leading organizations in the various fields of KM, BI, and CI. The cases reinforce some of the concepts presented in the first part of the book.

I am indebted to many people for their involvement with this book. First, let me thank my students and colleagues at Johns Hopkins University for their insight and support during this project. Second, I thank John Wyzalek, Karen Schober, and Kim Hackett at Auerbach Publications/Taylor & Francis for signing and producing this book (with special thanks to Andrea Demby). Third, a tremendous amount of gratitude is extended to all the authors of the case studies: Maritza Morales of Motorola, Inc.; Thomas Kern of the Annie E. Casey Foundation; Stephan Berwick of Northrop Grumman; Todd Drake, Bill McGilvery, and Liza Puterman of i2, a ChoicePoint Company; Shereen Remez of AARP; Francisco Cantu, Silvia Mora, Aldo Díaz, Héctor Ceballos, Sergio Martínez, and Daniel Jiménez of Tecnologico de Monterrey; Keith Johnston and Clint Gauvin of The Analysis Corporation; Peter McKenney of Cipher Systems LLC.; and Arik Johnson of Aurora WDC. I would also like to thank Doug Campbell of http://www.businessintelligence.com for allowing me to include some of my articles in this book.

And a final note of great appreciation goes to my family, Janet, Jason, and Kenny, who always support my endeavors with full enthusiasm.

Jay Liebowitz, D.Sc.
Washington, D.C.

CONCEPTS

I

Chapter 1

From Individual Transformation to Organizational Intelligence

Introduction

Change is omnipresent — nothing ever stays quite the same. Probing deeper usually reveals some element of change in what may appear to be unchanged on the surface. For example, the small town where you grew up may look like the same place that you remember — not much traffic, beautiful locale, same houses through proper upkeep, and the same nice townspeople. However, as you walk down the main street, you may notice that things really are not quite the same. The $1 movie theatre now charges $8. The leading and almost sole large employer has now moved most of its operations out of town. Many of the establishments on the main street are out of business due to the harsh economic situation. And even the old high school that you fondly remember has now been converted into a seniors' center.

Your hometown looks the same on the surface, but upon closer examination, reveals that change has taken place. The paradox "change is constant" is certainly true. But how can change be <u>constant</u>? Does not change indicate movement versus stillness? Or do we really mean that a constant rate of change exists, versus change vacillating unpredictably? We have also heard the expression "people never change." Is this quite true? There are certainly many events in life that may change a person. However, some believe that the genetic composition of an individual enforces a certain stability and pattern such that the environment may change, but the person never really changes.

The same argument is made for *knowledge management*. Knowledge management involves best leveraging knowledge internally and externally in an organization and creating a process for valuing the organization's intangible assets. Some people say that knowledge cannot be managed, i.e., the environment in which knowledge is housed, transferred, and used can change, but knowledge itself cannot be controlled. In this book, we ascribe to the philosophy that knowledge, as well as the environment itself, can be managed. We will come back to this notion in subsequent chapters.

Transformation

Have you ever been told that you are a *change agent?* You should be proud of this title, as it usually shows that you are influencing change in a positive way. For example, I have tried to bring about a change in my department at the university by making it fun to work there. Converting our conference table into a Ping-Pong table (that is, putting up a Ping-Pong net on our multipurpose conference table) has promoted a playful atmosphere in the department. Playing Ping-Pong together has helped create camaraderie among the administrators, faculty, staff, and students. Having "walking groups" at lunch, inviting students and faculty to homes for dinner, and even playing some harmless pranks in the office have helped transform the department culture into a less stodgy environment. In a sense, I hope that I have served as a change agent in transforming our department culture and forging a closer bond and community among ourselves, our students, and our administration and staff.

NASA introduced an Integrated Financial Management Program (IFMP) in its headquarters and across all NASA centers, which ultimately changed how the financial, human resources, contracting personnel, and project managers were used to working. After spending many years growing up with another approach to costing, a fundamental shift was being made in terms of financial management at NASA. To make this transition as smooth as possible, an IFMP change management program was introduced, and there were IFMP change agents throughout headquarters and the ten NASA centers. Besides having training courses on IFMP, these change agents regularly met with those affected and helped to reduce the anxiety of the unknown and to smoothly introduce the various modules of IFMP in a phased approach.

In discussing transformation, a fundamental question surfaces: do you have to first change the macro-level organizational culture before new initiatives (that may not fit the current organizational culture) can be introduced, or do you match the approach to the current organizational culture to achieve successful change at an individual level for possible incremental propagation at the organizational level? Simply put, do you need to change the culture first before introducing a new initiative? Authorities such as Edgar Schein and others have spent years studying organizational culture. As it could take 10 to 14 years to change a large organization's macro-culture, I believe that to get some quick wins, it is best to match an approach to the current organizational culture to succeed, rather than force-fitting an approach that goes against the macro-organizational culture. As people start to embrace the new initiative, some individual learning takes place that, over time, should lead to collective organizational learning and transformation.

Let us discuss some specifics so we can be clear on this issue. When I was the knowledge management officer at NASA Goddard Space Flight Center, I could have applied a codification strategy to knowledge management (a systems approach emphasizing the "collection" aspect of codifying tacit knowledge and making it explicit through systems), as well as a personalization strategy (people-to-people approach emphasizing "connections") for knowledge sharing. Usually, one approach will dominate another, but you should use a hybrid of knowledge management techniques. As most of the employees at Goddard were scientists, engineers, and technologists, they seemed to prefer a codification, systems approach, perhaps partly based on some aspects of introversion. To succeed in gaining acceptance of knowledge management, a codified approach seemed to fit the personalities of the individuals and the overarching culture. The application of an agencywide, lessons-learned information system (NASA has a lessons-learned information system at llis.nasa.gov) or developing a Goddard Web-based online searchable repository of videos, webcasts, images, and documents were examples of knowledge management projects that emphasized a codification approach. Of course, the use of expertise locator systems, knowledge-sharing forums in which expert and up-and-coming project managers would exchange "war stories," online communities of practice, and other personalization approaches were also used to push the "connections" piece of knowledge management.

In this example, the lesson learned was to match the knowledge management approach or solution that best fit the deployed organizational culture rather than trying to first change the culture of the organization and then introduce the knowledge management approach. Time and savings can be generated by this proper alignment of solution to culture.

Some, especially from the organizational learning community, may say that changing the culture must be done before injecting a new approach into the organization, because using an approach with the existing culture may perpetuate the same culture that currently exists. If you want organizations to change, this school of thought indicates that a top-down cultural shift is needed versus a bottom-up approach.

In examining knowledge management strategies with cultures, Juan Roman's 2003 dissertation (George Washington University) concluded that it is best to align knowledge management strategies with existing cultures (at least for government and not-for-profits) to better ensure knowledge management success. His dissertation demonstrated the value of this strategy.

Let us look at another example in which organizational transformation is a challenge. The Department of Homeland Security in the United States has about 177,000 employees from over 20 agencies. Each of these agencies has its own culture and "some play better with others." To share information and knowledge through various levels of the relatively new department, various cultural barriers have to be broken down. This is quite a tall order for trying to develop an integrated, cohesive department in which the whole is greater than the sum of its parts. However, for organizational intelligence to flourish within the department, there must be a massive cultural transformation to synergize the department. Instead of trying for a mass transformation of the large department, perhaps the subcultures of the component agencies working within the department could be addressed. In this manner, this transformational task may not be as daunting. However, the risk is that suboptimization may take place.

An analogy to this issue of changing the macro-organizational culture first before new initiatives can be introduced is throwing a large rock in the water and making a huge splash. In this manner, some say you must have a large impact first before organizational transformation can take place. Others say, as we do, that perhaps throwing a pebble in the water and having a ripple effect may be a better way to organizational transformation. In this manner, incremental improvement through individual learning can be accomplished, which can lead to overall organizational transformation.

What Do We Mean by Intelligence?

A key reason why organizational transformation is important is to increase the "intelligence" of the organization. *Organizational intelligence* refers

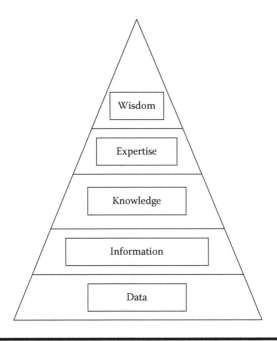

Figure 1.1   The intelligence hierarchy.

to the collective assemblage of value-added benefits derived from the organization's intangible assets (knowledge from employees, management, stakeholders, and customers). To increase the IQ of the organization, we should first build a hierarchy of components that contribute to the intelligence of an organization. The traditional hierarchy is shown in Figure 1.1.

Data relates to discerned elements. Once the data is patterned in some way, it becomes information. Information plus insights and experience becomes knowledge. Knowledge in a specialized area becomes expertise. Expertise morphs into the nirvana state of wisdom after many years of experience and lessons learned.

At an individual level, my sons sometimes say that they are more intelligent or smarter than I am. Although this may be true, my usual retort is that they may be smarter but not wiser. An analogy can be used here with respect to tennis. My children may have better tennis strokes than I do, but they still may lose because they have not yet mastered the "tennis strategy" whereby I have 30 more years of playing experience as an advantage. Similarly, people say that others may be book-smart, but not street-smart.

Knowledge and experience go hand-in-hand in developing intelligence, especially in an organizational setting. It reminds me of the first job that one tries to get where they want you to have experience first to get the job, but to gain experience, you must get that first job (the chicken and the egg phenomenon). Organizational intelligence, according to the knowledge management community, must be built on three main types of capital: human, structural, and relationship. *Human capital* refers to the knowledge embodied in the employees of the organization. *Structural capital* is the knowledge that you cannot easily take home with you from the office such as intellectual property rights, certain databases, and the like. *Relationship capital* is social capital learned from your customers and stakeholders. Some people say there is a fourth type of capital called *competitive capital*. This refers to the intelligence in knowing what your competitors are doing. For an organization to maximize its intelligence, all four types of capital must provide value-added benefits to the organization.

Let us now look at how change can affect organizational intelligence.

Vignette

What happens when there is too much change? What effect does it have on organizational intelligence? One large foundation was interested in applying knowledge management techniques to enhance its organizational intelligence and effectiveness. The foundation had a number of major business initiatives underway that dealt with automating the grant management process, establishing a foundation-wide strategic planning process, and engaging more actively in the community. Internally, in recent years, the organizational structure changed (merging, adding, and replacing departments), seemingly every four to six months. This caused tremendous stress on the employees as their job security was uncertain, a shifting of strategic and daily priorities was occurring frequently, and a sense of community among the foundation employees was eroding.

Why didn't the foundation just stabilize its organizational structure? Did this change have to be so frequent? The rate of change was so fast from an organizational perspective that turmoil resulted owing to an endless shifting of priorities. For knowledge management to be successful, the sense of community and level of trust in the organization typically needs to be strong. If not, people may be reluctant to share their knowledge and will become knowledge hoarders instead. This could then cause a reduction in the organizational intelligence as synergy will not take place due to a lack of knowledge sharing in the organization. Because of the frequent changes due to restructuring and the resulting lack of trust among employees and management, knowledge management has not taken hold in the foundation, and the potential for strengthening organizational intelligence has diminished.

The Effect of Culture on Organizational Intelligence

Culture may seem a nebulous term, but it has a strong bearing on an entity's organizational intelligence. When you walk down the hallway in a company and see the doors shut (even though you know that most people are in their closed offices), this connotes a type of culture that may seem "not open" or reluctant to have people stop in and share ideas. One department at a university had the Chairman's door closed all the time, so the faculty also thought it was permissible to keep their doors closed. This created an unfriendly culture among students, faculty, and staff as people seemed to hide. When the Chair was made aware of this phenomenon, she kept her door open and encouraged the faculty and staff to follow suit. This created a more symbiotic culture whereby people felt easier about chatting with colleagues and interacting with students. The same department first had a bulletin board, right in front of the elevators, with the names of the faculty categorized by rank. When it was pointed out that this promoted a hierarchical view of the department, as opposed to a collegial associative perspective, the bulletin board was changed to list the faculty alphabetically (with their ranks appearing after their names).

All of these actions affect the culture in the organization. Closed doors–open doors, hierarchical–collegial — these have a bearing on how people interact in the organization and how outsiders and stakeholders view the organization. People dressing business–casual every day in the office as the accepted organization dress norm versus having everyone dress in business suits or equivalent attire also affects the organizational culture.

How does culture then influence organizational intelligence? If organizational intelligence includes human capital, then how employees perceive themselves and how they fit into the organizational environment can dramatically affect the growth or decline of human capital. Let us take an example. Suppose you are a very creative person who does not like to deal with the bureaucracies and rules that may be enforced upon you in your hierarchical, very structured organization. And let us suppose your boss is a very controlling person who likes to micromanage his subordinates. It probably would be difficult for you to cope very long and thrive in this kind of a constrained environment, especially if you like doing your own thing. Your creativity may be hampered in this climate or culture, which would probably diminish your innovation and productivity. Your human capital growth, especially your organization's human capital and intelligence, would decline due to your feeling uncomfortable in this type of environment.

According to Dave DeLong, in his book titled *Lost Knowledge: Confronting the Threat of an Aging Workforce* (Oxford University Press, 2004), a culture's support for knowledge retention can be determined by the levels of trust in the organization, which is often reflected in a shared sense of purpose. Organizational intelligence can be enhanced if there is a knowledge-sharing culture in the organization versus people suppressing their knowledge. However, as we mentioned earlier, if the culture does not encourage people to share what they know, then they will retain the knowledge to themselves. Thus, having high levels of trust in the organization should help nurture and increase the organizational intelligence. As DeLong points out, Delta Air Lines asked more than 50 high-performing employees who were leaving voluntarily to share their knowledge and explain different aspects of their jobs with others before leaving the company. Delta Air Lines held luncheons to recognize and thank these individuals for their service and for participating in this knowledge transfer program. This resonated very well with the remaining employees of Delta and helped sustain trust levels and build support for other knowledge retention activities. In this case, culture again (through trust) affected the organizational intelligence by facilitating a knowledge-sharing atmosphere to create synergies.

Change Management Processes

As organizations transform themselves through cultural and paradigm shifts, change management processes must be introduced and skillfully integrated within the daily work activities of the individual. Similarly, for knowledge management to be successful, such activities must be embedded within the normal routines at the workplace. For example, for lessons learned to be captured and used at NASA, the NASA program and project management guidelines state that the project teams must capture and apply lessons learned throughout the project development life cycle. When a NASA project team would be reviewed, the review chairs could ask how lessons learned were captured from their project and what value-added benefits the project team derived from accessing the existing lessons learned. The lessons-learned process has become part of the NASA project management process — not something that the NASA project team member will do if he or she gets around to it.

For organizations to transform, change management processes are mandatory not voluntary. We have seen that business process reengineering (BPR), business process improvement (BPI), Total Quality Management (TQM), customer relationship management (CRM), and other management techniques must encompass a change management element to be successful. Some organizations have learned this lesson the hard way by using the "over-the-wall phenomenon," in which you throw a new system or approach over the wall and hope that someone catches it on the other side. In the IT field, a change management strategy is sometimes overlooked as it seems to be more ephemeral than building the system itself. The change management strategy should be considered up front at the beginning of the system development life cycle and should be part of the implementation strategy. If the IT project team, as part of the requirements stage, does not start thinking about how business processes may have to be reengineered when the resulting system is introduced, then it may be too late for the IT system to be successful. Whether it is automating the grant proposal submission and review process, automating how customers interact with the company, or the like, change management processes have to be carefully considered up front in the overall planning stage.

Strategy and change are intrinsically linked. What happened to the railroad industry years ago when it thought it was merely in the railroad business and not the transportation business? The railroad industry lost a major part of its consumer base because it did not adapt to the changing perceptions of the consumers and to competing industries. What happened to EuroDisney (Disneyland Paris) when Disney tried to impose American customs on the French workers and management? It was a disaster; Disney lost a tremendous amount of revenue, and employee morale was extremely low. Strategy and change management go hand-in-hand, and change management processes must be embedded within the organizational fabric for strategy shifts to be successful.

Improved strategy and change management processes will enhance organizational intelligence. In the following chapters, we will look at the various types of intelligentsia, and we will show that strategic intelligence is the synergy between knowledge management, business intelligence, and competitive intelligence.

Chapter 2

Intelligentsia Galore

Introduction

In Chapter 1, we defined *organizational intelligence* as the collective assemblage of value-added benefits derived from the organization's intangible assets. We discussed that culture, change management, and individual transformation are, among others, important components leading to organizational transformation and a heightened organizational intelligence. However, wherever you turn, a new type of "xyz intelligence" emerges — artificial intelligence (AI), business intelligence (BI), competitive intelligence (CI), and the list goes on.

Is there any way to consolidate and synthesize the various types of intelligentsia into a meaningful framework? Figure 2.1 shows how some of these intelligentsia relate to each other. The inner layer refers to AI. This is the field of developing intelligent systems to support or, in some cases, replace the decision maker. AI refers to how to build intelligent computer power to supplement our human brain power. It also looks at how learning, thinking, explaining, and other cognitive processes take place. Typical applications of AI are expert or knowledge-based systems, natural language processing, case-based reasoning, speech understanding, robotics, computer vision, neural networks, genetic algorithms, and hybrid intelligent systems. Even though we are including AI as the inner layer of our intelligentsia framework, we are not saying that all knowledge management (KM), BI, CI, and strategic intelligence (SI) must therefore include AI applications and techniques. We are saying that many of the AI techniques could be useful in these other intelligentsia (such as knowledge representation techniques for developing knowledge ontologies or

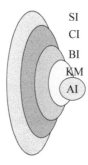

SI
CI
BI
KM
AI

Figure 2.1 A framework of intelligentsia.

case-based reasoning for help desk applications or business rule engines); however, most of these other intelligentsia do not necessarily use AI in practice.

Because AI deals with how we think, it seems only natural that KM should embrace some of these concepts to help people capture, organize, and share knowledge within the organization and externally with the stakeholders. Thus, KM is the next layer of the intelligentsia onion. KM looks at how an organization can best leverage its knowledge to innovate, retain critical "at-risk" knowledge, build camaraderie and a strong sense of belonging, and improve worker productivity. Besides knowledge, an organization must deal with using information effectively. According to Jean Schauer's article, "The Next Evolution in Business Intelligence" (*DM Review*, October 2004), the aforementioned is the definition for BI. Rob Ashe, President and CEO of Cognos (*DM Review*, October 2004), feels that BI is really dealing with corporate performance management (CPM) in terms of improving organizational decision making. Ashe feels that BI and CPM allow organizations to align execution with strategy. BI forms the next layer of the intelligentsia onion after KM, and then CI becomes the next layer by using both internal and external information and knowledge to develop a systematic and ethical program to manage, analyze, and apply this information and know-how for improving organizational decision making. Finally, the aggregation of all these various intelligentsia becomes SI for the organization to best make strategic decisions. According to a study of U.K. executives (Xu et al., 2003), business environment scanning contributes greatly to SI gathering. This research indicated that U.K. executives perceive the immediate-task environment information to be more strategically important than far-general environment information. In addition, the far-general information perceptions vary widely between industries. This might also suggest that another type of intelligence exists, namely "customer intelligence." Computer Sciences Corporation (www.csc.com) feels that organizations must drive business results through the strategic use of customer intelligence. For our purposes, we include customer intelligence as being the social, relationship, or customer capital in our KM definition.

Let us now take a closer look at the synergies that could be derived from the integration of these various types of intelligentsia.

Artificial Intelligence

The field of AI has been around since 1956 when it was coined at the Dartmouth Conference. The focus of AI has been to better understand how we think, learn, and reason, and to develop computer programs that can assist or emulate us in well-defined tasks. Some people feel that AI should have been called intelligence amplification (IA) to stress the importance of the decision maker's (i.e., human's) role in the decision-making process. Instead of concentrating on ways to replace humans, some say the focus should have been on supporting the decision maker and keeping him/her in the loop.

For practical purposes other than the AI subfield of robotics, the emphasis of AI has been in the decision support mode. For example, knowledge-based or expert systems have been developed in many areas, from medicine to business to agriculture, to help in the decision-making process. Even though the eventual goal was to develop an expert system to replace the human expert for well-defined tasks, many of the expert systems developed were built as a decision support aide.

The development process for expert systems is called *knowledge engineering*. There are many similarities between the knowledge engineering process and the KM process. Knowledge engineering consists of the following steps: problem selection, knowledge acquisition, knowledge representation, knowledge encoding, knowledge testing and evaluation, and implementation/operations and maintenance. KM consists of knowledge identification and capture, knowledge sharing, knowledge application, and knowledge creation. Knowledge elicitation and knowledge representation techniques from the knowledge engineering community should be applied to the KM development process in terms of capturing knowledge and developing knowledge ontologies. Certainly, the rapid prototyping approach used in knowledge engineering should also be applied in KM applications in terms of the "build a little, test a little" approach. Additionally, the incentives and recognition structures used to determine why an expert would want his or her knowledge to be encoded in an expert system could also parallel why people would want to share their competitive edge. Additionally, as many KM applications capture lessons learned and best practices, expert systems capture the heuristics (rules of thumb acquired from experience) and set of facts relating to a well-defined domain of knowledge (the set of facts and heuristics comprise the *knowledge base* of the expert system).

Neural networks are another application of AI. They deal with emulating interconnected webs of neurons similar to how our brain works. They are typically used in applications that have "noisy data," that is, problem areas that deal with data fluctuations such as signal processing, image understanding, credit card fraud detection, etc. Unlike expert systems, which are a white box approach, neural networks are more of a black box approach to computation. With expert systems, the explanation capabilities and the inference engine allow the user to view the rules that are being fired to arrive at an intermediate or final conclusion. With neural networks, there are mathematical manipulations of weights and summation functions that do not easily lend themselves to being understood by the user (thus, the black box notation). However, even though neural networks can be automatically worked on without human intervention, the results of the neural networks can be reviewed by a human for the final decision making.

Other applications of AI, including speech understanding, natural language processing, genetic algorithms, data/text mining, and computer vision, are also active fields of research and commercial usage. Certainly, data and text mining can uncover hidden patterns and relationships of large masses of data and text that could help the KM field in creating knowledge. These techniques could be used in link analysis and be applied to social network analysis for determining knowledge flows and gaps in organizations. It seems apparent that many aspects of AI should be an integral part of KM.

Knowledge Management

With the population "graying" and organizations facing potential knowledge drains, the advent and importance of KM and strategic human capital management play critical roles for society. KM deals with creating a process for generating value from an organization's intangible assets. Simply put, as mentioned in Chapter 1, KM is how to best leverage knowledge internally and externally. According to Dave DeLong's (2004) book on *Lost Knowledge: Confronting the Threat of an Aging Workforce*, "knowledge retention will become an overriding concern in the years ahead in sectors such as government, manufacturing, energy, healthcare, education, and aerospace." Many organizations have embraced KM as part of their human capital strategy. For example, the U.S. Office of Personnel

Management has a "Leadership and Knowledge Management" pillar as part of their recommended strategic management of human capital framework for government organizations. As part of building a human capital strategy for the organization, several key pillars should be included — competency management, performance management, change management, and KM. As I point out in my book, *Addressing the Human Capital Crisis in the Federal Government: A Knowledge Management Perspective* (Elsevier, 2004), these are the fundamental structures underpinning a human capital strategy. Competency management deals with the skills and knowledge areas required for the organization's workforce of the future. Performance management relates to the recognition and reward structure associated with achieving some desired level of worker or organizational performance. Change management, often the overlooked pillar, deals with transforming the organization from a state of individualized learning to collective learning. This, as we previously discussed in the first chapter, is where KM can play a role.

A number of researchers and practitioners have been studying techniques and methodologies for developing KM strategies and implementation plans. According to Chourides et al. (2003), to get anywhere with KM, you must have a strategy and individuals must be persuaded to contribute to both formulation and implementation. The KM strategic plan has greater focus on the knowledge needs of the organization and an evaluation of capabilities. Apostolou and Mentzas (2003) developed the Know-Net KM approach, which includes the interplay between strategy, assets, processes, systems, structures, individuals, teams, interorganizations, and the organization itself. Sveiby (2001) discusses his knowledge-based theory of the firm and indicates nine knowledge strategy questions:

1. How can we improve the transfer of competence between people in our organization?
2. How can the organization's employees improve the competence of customers, suppliers, and other stakeholders?
3. How can the organization's customers, suppliers, and other stakeholders improve the competence of the employees?
4. How can we improve the conversion of individually held competence to systems, tools, and templates?
5. How can we improve individual competence by using systems, tools, and templates?
6. How can we enable the conversations among the customers, suppliers, and stakeholders so they improve their competence?
7. How can competence from the customers, suppliers, and other stakeholders improve the organization's systems, tools, processes, and products?

8. How can the organization's systems, tools, processes, and products improve the competence of the customers, suppliers, and other stakeholders?
9. How can the organization's systems, tools, processes, and products be effectively integrated?

O'Dell et al. (1999) have performed benchmarking studies on KM strategies. They have found organizations using KM strategies as a matrix of KM as a business strategy, transfer of knowledge and best practices, customer-focused knowledge, personal responsibility for knowledge, intellectual asset management, and innovation and knowledge creation. Levett and Guenov (2000) have developed a methodology for KM implementation that looks at a four-phase approach of case-study definition: capture KM practice, build a KM strategy, and implement and evaluate. April (2002) has developed guidelines for building a knowledge strategy looking at the interlinking of assets or resources, complementary resource combinations, and the strategic architecture of the company. Nickerson and Silverman (1998) have examined intellectual capital management strategies and proposed a strategy integration analysis methodology that uses six steps: assemble a multidisciplinary team, identify and select a target market and position, identify investments and technology, identify unique or idiosyncratic technologies that form the basis of competitive advantage by comparing the firm's technology and intellectual position with that of potential competitors, choose optimal organizational and intellectual capital management configuration based on the preceding four steps, and evaluate expected profitability of this integrated strategy. Other researchers and practitioners such as McElroy (2003), Mertins et al. (2001), Hult (2003), Davenport and Probst (2002), NASA KM Team (2001), Liebowitz et al. (in press), and Zimmermann (2003) have been involved in writing case studies dealing with KM strategy and implementations.

From the American Productivity and Quality Center's Knowledge Management Benchmarking studies (2000), the key features of successful implementation of KM are:

- An important senior champion or group saw the strategic value of KM and endorsed what became a significant investment in it.
- Communities of practice are a central part of the KM strategy. Sponsorship, membership, roles and responsibilities, accountability and measurement, and supporting tools are the elements that must be in place to develop and evolve communities.
- Functional silos are the most significant cultural barrier to KM implementation. Solicit senior leadership vision and active support to break down these barriers.

- The importance of making connections — of people to people and of people to information — is the driver to use information technology (IT) in KM initiatives.
- As KM becomes more structured and widespread, the need for measurement steadily increases.

Seeley and Dietrick (2001) discuss building a KM strategy using the following components: governance, culture, content management, technology, application, and measurement. Earl (2001) discusses a knowledge mapping, cartographic approach to KM, in which knowledge networking and incentives to share knowledge are critical success factors. AT&T and Bain and Company use this approach. Chavel and Despres (2002) in their 1997–2001 review of survey research in KM found that surveys are typically used in KM research. Liebowitz (2004) discusses the importance of KM as a key pillar in an organization's human capital strategy. Holsapple (2003), Wexler (2001), Noll et al. (2002), Hylton (2003), and Grey (1999) talk about the importance of performing a knowledge audit as a first step in developing a KM strategy for an organization.

Most of the current research in addressing KM strategies and implementations has focused on ad hoc approaches. Unfortunately, without the necessary rigor behind these approaches, KM will become the "management fad of the day" and will fall into demise (similar to the 70% failure rate estimated in business process reengineering projects). Part of what is needed to further advance the KM field and to give senior management a stronger sense of trust in the "tangible" advantages of KM in their organizations is a comprehensive KM maturity (KMM) model. This KMM model would allow a structured methodology for KM development and strategy formulation to ensure greater success of KM implementation efforts. Siemens has a KMM model, based on the CMMI model developed at the Software Engineering Institute at Carnegie-Mellon University, but other KMM models should also be developed and explored (Ehms and Langen, 2002; Marco, 2002). According to Pelz-Sharpe and Harris-Jones' (2005) article on "KM: Past and Future," "we expect to see over the next 18 months, the reemergence of KM in the workplace."

Business Intelligence

I see BI having a more internal focus than CI. BI has been defined a myriad of ways, but I like the "Knowledge Management and Business Intelligence (KMBI) Workshop" definition. They define BI as an "active, model-based, and prospective approach to discover and explain hidden, decision-relevant aspects in large amounts of business data to better inform business decision processes" (KMBI, 2005). Through this definition, you can see the synergies between KM and AI/data mining.

According to the Gartner Group's "Predicts 2004" report on BI and data warehousing, they found that (1) many organizations in 2004 were concentrating on formulating enterprise-wide BI strategies and applying best practices and (2) the softer side of BI (skills and planning issues relating to successful BI implementations) is a key focal point for many organizations. The Gartner Group "BI Software Market: Europe 2000–2007" report indicated that new BI software license revenue will rise from $579 million in 2003 to $823 million in 2007 in Europe.

BI implementations can learn from KM implementations. According to Raub and von Wittich's (2004) research, the critical success factors for KM implementation are: aligning the contributions of key organizational actors, promoting the development of knowledge networks, and providing support by delivering a purposeful message. These critical success factors can also be applied to BI. Key senior sponsorship, expanded presence, and a value-added message are all important elements for BI usage.

Looking toward the future of BI, Betts (2004) believes that BI will mean more people viewing more data in more detail. Betts feels that more companies will be putting BI tools into the hands of the typical employee, not just the marketing or financial analyst. Additionally, unstructured data, predictive analytics, and integration will be key trends that will exist in the BI domain. Others feel that the corporate information factory (CIF) is the way of the future and that BI has a major role to play. According to Claudia Imhoff (WatchIT.com, 2004), the CIF is the architecture that supports BI. In this CIF, there are business operations, BI, and business management. The role of BI is to provide the systems that supply the corporation with the trends, patterns, exceptions, and analytical capabilities to determine these patterns (WatchIT.com, 2004).

KM techniques can enhance BI. As organizations continue to develop their enterprise-wide BI strategies, KM should be an integral part of their plans.

Competitive Intelligence

Helen Rothberg and Scott Erickson (2005), in their book *From Knowledge to Intelligence: Creating Competitive Advantage in the Next Economy*, discuss the adage that "knowledge has value, intelligence has power." In view of this recurring theme in their book, they indicate that CI is finding what you need by using what you know. Rothberg and Erickson (2005) discuss the notion of generating competitive capital and knowing if your organization is on the right path toward doing so by being able to answer the following three questions:

1. Do you know all of what you need to know before making a strategic decision?
2. Do you know where to find what you need to know?
3. Do you know what to do with the information once you find it?

The answers to these questions certainly build upon the type of KM systems that are available to the organization. Bret Breeding, of Shell Services International (2001), talks about the convergence of CI and KM. The marriage and synergy between these two areas help to determine the knowledge flows and gaps to better assess where you are, what you need to know, and how best to find out.

I see CI having both internal and external components; thus, that is why BI (with its internal focus) is subsumed within CI. CI is used to solve both short-term and long-term problems, whereas KM is more likely to be used for a long-term perspective on derived benefits. According to a 2004 survey of CI professionals conducted by SIS International Research (Klein, 2004), consulting was the most popular industry for performing and using CI. Other highly rated industries included market research, financial services, manufacturing, software, telecommunications, pharmaceuticals, and healthcare. The survey also showed the greatest value from CI is strategic planning. The survey indicated the top four unmet needs of CI practitioners as being: (1) tying CI to the bottom line, (2) education and training, (3) finding information, and (4) knowing how to apply CI for maximum advantage.

CI is closely linked with BI, KM, and AI. Similar to its other intelligentsia, CI has a gathering, analysis, and management component. CI has an internal and external focus, and relies heavily on external information for the CI analyst to base his or her opinions. CI also relies on a number of established methodologies for information and knowledge collection, analysis, and management. For example, scenario building is often done in the CI community for forecasting external and internal trends looking 3 to 5 years out and beyond. In this manner, changes in environmental conditions affecting the organization can be anticipated, and various scenarios can be developed to determine how the organization can best prepare for these new situations.

According to the Society of Competitive Intelligence Professionals (www.scip.org), the CI professional is an important part of an organization's workforce and can be located in numerous departments within the organization — a CI department, strategy planning, business development, product development, research and development, marketing research and analysis, human resources, etc. The key purpose of CI is to keep the organization well-informed and to be able to prepare in advance to anticipate challenges so that the organization can continue to thrive and flourish. It forms a symbiotic relationship with strategic planning, as it provides the key inputs to help steer the strategic planning process for the organization. Without it, the organization would drift and the adage "if you do not know where you are going, any road will do" would become reality. Thus, CI, similar to the other inherent types of intelligentsia, should be used to help crystallize what might be called SI.

Strategic Intelligence

SI is the aggregation of the other types of intelligentsia to provide value-added information and knowledge toward making organizational strategic decisions. SI is often used in the military or defense world to signify information or knowledge that can be helpful for high-level decision making. This is often distinguished from operational or tactical intelligence, which are lower-level types of intelligence. In the business setting, SI has a similar meaning as that under the military intelligence vogue, but the emphasis is on how best to position the organization to deal with future challenges and opportunities to maximize the firm's success.

SI forms the outer layer of the onion, with the inside layers being AI, KM, BI, and CI. KM does not necessarily have to include AI applications, although in many areas, AI could greatly support and enhance KM. In the following chapters, you will learn about the KM, BI, and CI layers and how they fold neatly into SI.

References

American Productivity and Quality Center, Successfully Implementing Knowledge Management, Best practice report, Houston, TX, 2000.

Apostolou, D. and Mentzas, G. Experiences from knowledge management implementations in companies of the software sector, *Business Process Management Journal*, Vol. 9, No. 3, 2003.

April, K. Guidelines for developing a k-strategy, *Journal of Knowledge Management*, Vol. 6, No. 5, 2002.

Betts, M., The future of business intelligence, *Computerworld*, June 21, 2004.

Breeding, B., CI and KM convergence: a case study at Shell Services International, *Proven Strategies in Competitive Intelligence: Lessons from the Trenches*, Prescott, J. and Miller, S., Eds., John Wiley & Sons, New York, 2001.

Chauvel, D. and Despres, C., A review of survey research in knowledge management: 1997–2001, *Journal of Knowledge Management*, Vol. 6, No. 3, 2002.

Chourides, P., Longbottom, D., and Murphy, W., Excellence in knowledge management: an empirical study to identify critical factors and performance measures, *Measuring Business Excellence*, Vol. 7, No. 2, 2003.

Davenport, T. and Probst G. (Eds.), *Knowledge Management Case Book: Siemens Best Practices*, 2nd ed., John Wiley & Sons/Publicis Corporate Publishing, Berlin, 2002.

DeLong, D., *Lost Knowledge: Confronting the Threat of an Aging Workforce*, Oxford University Press, New York, 2004.

Earl, M., Knowledge management strategies: toward a taxonomy, *Journal of Management Information Systems*, Vol. 18, No. 1, Summer 2001.

Ehms, K. and Langen, M., Holistic Development of Knowledge Management with KMMM, 2002, http://www.knowledgeboard.com/doclibrary/knowledge-board/kmmm_article_siemens_2002.pdf.

Grey, D. Knowledge Mapping: A Practical Overview, March 1999, http://www.it-consultancy.com/extern/sws/knowmap.html.

Holsapple, C., *Handbook on Knowledge Management*, 2 Volumes, Springer-Verlag, Heidelberg, 2003.

Hult, G.T., An integration of thoughts on knowledge management, *Decision Sciences*, Vol. 34, No. 2, Spring 2003.

Hylton, A., The knowledge audit, *Proceedings of the Knowledge Management Aston Conference 2003*, Edwards, J., Ed., The Operational Research Society/Aston Business School, Birmingham, U.K., 2003.

Klein, S., CI international market assessment: research findings, *Competitive Intelligence Magazine*, Society of Competitive Intelligence Professionals, Alexandria, VA, Vol. 7, No. 5, September–October 2004.

Knowledge Management and Business Intelligence (KMBI) Workshop, http://wm2005.iese.fraunhofer.de, Germany, April 2005.

Levett, G. and Guenov, M., A methodology for knowledge management implementation, *Journal of Knowledge Management*, Vol. 4, No. 3, 2000.

Liebowitz, J., Holm, J., and Day, R. (Eds.) (in press), Making Sense out of Rocket Science: Managing Knowledge at NASA, Washington, D.C.

Liebowitz, J., *Addressing the Human Capital Crisis in the Federal Government: A Knowledge Management Perspective*, Butterworth-Heinemann/Elsevier, Boston, MA, 2004.

Marco, D., Meta Data and Knowledge Management: Capability Maturity Model: An Introduction, 2002, http://www.dmreview.com/editorial/dmreview/print_action.cfm?articleID=5567.

McElroy, M., *The New Knowledge Management*, Butterworth-Heinemann/Elsevier, Burlington, MA, 2003.

Mertins, K., Heisig, P., and Vorbeck, J. (Eds.), *Knowledge Management: Best Practices in Europe*, Springer-Verlag, Heidelberg, 2001

NASA Knowledge Management Team, Strategic Plan for Knowledge Management, Washington, D.C., March 18, 2001.

Nickerson, J. and Silverman, B., Intellectual capital management strategy: the foundation of successful new business generation, *Journal of Knowledge Management*, Vol. 1, No. 4, 1998.

Noll, M., Frohlich, D., and Schiebel, E., Knowledge Maps of Knowledge Management Tools: Information Visualization with BibTechMon, *Practical Applications of Knowledge Management 2002 Conference Proceedings*, Karagiannis, D. and Reimer, U., Eds., Springer-Verlag, Heidelberg, 2002.

O'Dell, C., Wiig, K., and Odem, P., Benchmarking unveils emerging knowledge management strategies, *Benchmarking Journal*, Vol. 6, No. 3, 1999.

Pelz-Sharpe, A. and Harris-Jones, C., KM: past and future, *KM World*, January 2005.

Raub, S. and von Wittich, D., Implementing KM: three strategies for effective chief knowledge officers, *European Management Journal*, Vol. 22, No. 6, 2004.

Rothberg, H. and Scott Erickson, G., *From Knowledge to Intelligence: Creating Competitive Advantage in the Next Economy*, Butterworth-Heinemann/Elsevier, Boston, MA, 2005.

Seeley, C. and Dietrick, W., Crafting a Knowledge Management Strategy, KM review special report, Melcrum Publishing, London, 2001.

Sveiby, K.E., A knowledge-based theory of the firm to guide in strategy formulation, *Journal of Intellectual Capital*, Vol. 2, No. 4, 2001.

WatchIT.com, Delivering Business Intelligence: Getting the Most from Your Storage Area Networks, Interview with Claudia Imhoff, 2004.

Wexler, M., The who, what, and why of knowledge mapping, *Journal of Knowledge Management*, Vol. 5, 2001.

Xu, X., Kaye R., and Duan Y., UK executives' vision on business environment for information scanning: a cross-industry study, *Information and Management Journal*, Elsevier, Vol. 40, 2003.

Zimmermann, K., Learning from success and failure, *KM World*, October 2003, www.kmworld.com.

Chapter 3

Organizational Intelligence through Strategic Intelligence: The Synergy of Knowledge Management, Competitive Intelligence, and Business Intelligence

Introduction

Over recent years, a synergy of business intelligence (BI), competitive intelligence (CI), and knowledge management (KM) has contributed to the formation and development of strategic intelligence (SI). Organizations need to apply these catalysts to foster SI for improved decision making. By doing so, the IQ of the organization should grow and the organization's institutional memory will be preserved and strengthened.

When looking at an organization's intelligence, there are four general types of capital that can be harnessed and nurtured. The first is *human capital*, which is the brainpower of your employees (essentially, the knowledge that your employees possess). *Structural capital* is the second type, which refers to the knowledge gained from things you cannot easily take home with you from the office, like intellectual property rights. The third type of capital is *customer capital* (sometimes referred to as *social* or *relationship capital*). This is the knowledge gained from your customers and stakeholders, and you incorporate this knowledge into your own organization's knowledge base. The last main type of capital is called *competitive capital*, which is the knowledge gained from your competitors. These four main types of knowledge will help an organization determine its IQ or intellectual capital.

In this chapter, we will use an actual case study that shows how KM, in particular, can contribute to the organization's intelligence.

Case Study of JL (a Pseudonym): Introduction

One of the key strategic themes for JL is "sharing knowledge." As such, knowledge-sharing and KM activities should play increasingly important roles in JL in the years ahead. To develop a KM strategy for JL, a knowledge audit (Liebowitz, 2000; Liebowitz, 2004; Annie E. Casey Foundation, 2003a; Annie E. Casey Foundation, 2003b) has been conducted as a critical first step toward helping construct a KM strategy for JL.

JL has recognized the importance of KM in its quest to become a "learning organization." KM has proven to be a strategic and value-added endeavor for improving an organization's effectiveness. For example, according to the American Productivity and Quality Center (2002), Chevron had a $2 billion reduction in annual operating costs through its communities of practice and transfer of best practices. Cap Gemini Ernst and Young had a tenfold growth in revenue with a fivefold increase in employees through use of communities of practice, central knowledge managers, and content management. Schlumberger used their technical communities of practice, intranet, and portal to save $75 million in their first year of these KM activities, with $100 million projected customer savings.

The Knowledge Audit Process at JL

After reviewing various knowledge audit surveys and through the experience of the author, a knowledge audit survey instrument was developed for JL via iterations and successive refinements with the management and staff. We received a 43 percent response rate with 36 surveys completed out of 83 possible employees. Even though it would have been better to achieve a higher response rate, Hylton (2003) indicates that a 30 percent response rate for a knowledge audit is acceptable. We were able to receive a representative sample of respondents across divisions as well as based on the employee length of time at JL.

In addition to the survey responses, follow-up interviews (JL, 2003) were conducted with key individuals in JL. Sample questions used during the interviews generally covered the following topics depending upon the individual interviewed:

1. What do you feel are the core competencies of JL?
2. What do you feel are some of the challenges facing JL in terms of meeting its strategic mission and vision?
3. In what ways do you feel that KM and knowledge-sharing activities can help meet your strategic mission and vision?
4. Do you feel there are any critical "at-risk" knowledge areas within JL in which core competency knowledge may be lost due to the expert leaving/retiring in one to three years and no backup expert exists? If so, what would be these "at-risk" knowledge areas, and who are the experts?
5. On a scale of 1 (low) to 10 (high), how would you rate these knowledge areas being strategic to JL's mission?
6. When you have a question, what is generally your first action in attempting to resolve it (i.e., talk with a colleague, look at a document, search the Web/intranet, etc.)?
7. For work-related questions in your area of responsibility, who are the top three people you might normally speak with to resolve these questions?
8. For non-work-related questions, who are the top three people in JL or elsewhere that you would ask for advice?
9. What keeps you up at night relating to work issues?
10. What are the biggest constraints in being able to perform your daily work?

Knowledge Audit Results

The following figures (Figure 3.1 to Figure 3.4) display some of the results from the knowledge audit survey. Analysis of the findings will be presented in the following section.

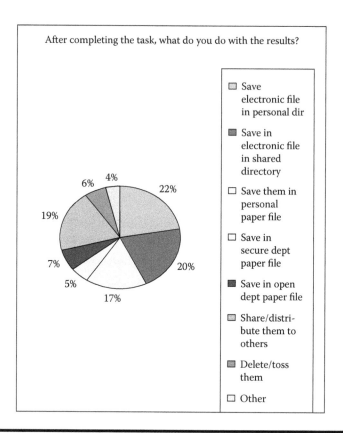

After completing the task, what do you do with the results?

- ☐ Save electronic file in personal dir
- ■ Save in electronic file in shared directory
- ☐ Save them in personal paper file
- ☐ Save in secure dept paper file
- ■ Save in open dept paper file
- ▨ Share/distribute them to others
- ▨ Delete/toss them
- ☐ Other

22%
20%
17%
5%
7%
19%
6%
4%

Figure 3.1   What happens to results after job is completed?

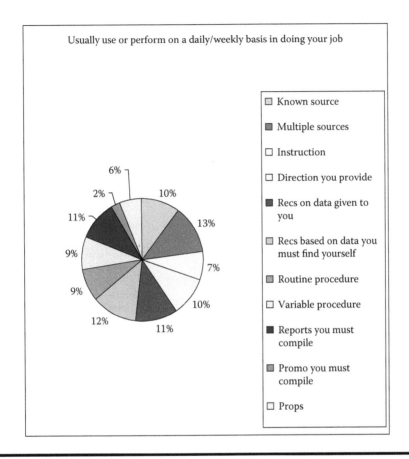

Figure 3.2 Frequency and tools used to perform job.

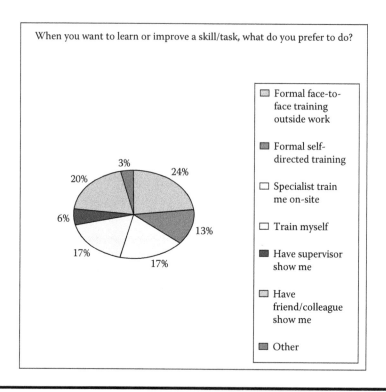

When you want to learn or improve a skill/task, what do you prefer to do?

□ Formal face-to-face training outside work

■ Formal self-directed training

□ Specialist train me on-site

□ Train myself

■ Have supervisor show me

□ Have friend/colleague show me

■ Other

Figure 3.3   Methods for learning or improving a skill or task.

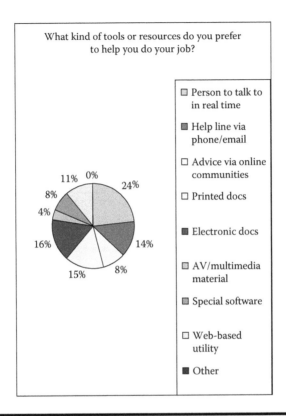

Figure 3.4   Preferred tools or resources.

How often on average do you ask each of the following staff for help with understanding or clarifying how you are to perform your job, solving a problem, getting an answer to a question from a grantee or customer, or learning how to accomplish a new task?

Table 3.1 Frequency Staff Is Asked for Help

	Daily	*Weekly*	*Monthly*	*Quarterly*	*Never*
Your immediate supervisor	25%	71%	4%	0%	0%
Your department head	23%	55%	18%	4%	0%
Your division head	0%	24%	36%	12%	28%
Subject matter expert (in an area of policy, practice, or research)	11%	33%	30%	15%	11%
Technical or functional expert (e.g., accounting, legal, grants administration, technology)	11%	54%	29%	7%	0%
A peer or colleague in your department or division (informal)	46%	35%	15%	4%	0%
A peer or colleague outside your department or division (informal)	14%	39%	39%	7%	0%

How often on average do you use each of the following to do your job?

Table 3.2 Frequency and Tools Used to Perform Job

	Daily	*Weekly*	*Monthly*	*Quarterly*	*Never*
JL-wide database	36%	29%	11%	7%	18%
JL-operated Web site	50%	43%	7%	0%	0%
Department- or division-operated database (e.g., shared calendar)	20%	20%	20%	8%	32%
My own database or contact list file	62%	31%	7%	0%	0%
JL policy/procedures manual or guidelines	4%	18%	39%	39%	0%
Department- or division-specific procedures manual or guidelines	7%	15%	18%	15%	44%
Vendor-provided procedures manual or guidelines	0%	8%	12%	40%	40%
My own notes or procedures	48%	41%	7%	0%	4%

To what extent do you agree with the following statements:

Table 3.3   Survey Results

	Strongly Disagree	Disagree	No Opinion	Agree	Strongly Agree
I would benefit from having access to documents that contain introductory knowledge that I currently have to acquire from experts directly.	4%	14%	11%	39%	32%
I would benefit from templates to help me more easily capture knowledge (e.g., standard format for documenting what I learned at a conference or meeting).	4%	11%	14%	43%	28%
I would benefit from processes to help me contribute knowledge that I don't currently document or share.	4%	11%	15%	37%	33%
I would benefit from support to determine the most relevant knowledge to share for various audiences and how best to share it.	4%	4%	30%	41%	22%
I have knowledge in areas that I know JL could benefit from but no (easy or obvious) way to make it available.	4%	19%	38%	27%	11%

Analysis of the Findings Based on the Knowledge Audit Survey

Knowledge Resources

The survey results indicate that people prefer (42 percent) to e-mail or talk with a JL colleague as their first choice in looking for information. The clear second course of action is to perform a global Web search (31 percent), typically using Google, and 18 percent will search online JL resources. This suggests two key findings. First, JL staff prefers the personalization approach — that is, the people-to-people connections. This is further evidenced by having the largest percentage (46 percent) of respondents indicate that they seek informal help from a peer or colleague in their department or division on a daily basis. Encouraging personalization approaches through knowledge-sharing forums, storytelling at staff meetings, brown-bag lunches, shadowing, mentoring, and use of face-to-face and online communities should be part of the JL's KM strategy. There is also additional evidence that JL staff follow a hierarchical pattern when seeking advice from others. For example, the immediate supervisor's help is sought 71 percent of the time on a weekly basis; the department head's help is 55 percent on a weekly basis; and the division head's help is 24 percent on a weekly basis. Culturally (and as expressed in the JL organizational chart), the JL staff have a hierarchical view of the organization; however, the cross-teaming used in the strategic business initiatives (SBI) should help cut across functional silos and hierarchies.

The second finding regarding knowledge resources is that people will often use the Web search via Google as the means for locating information and answers to their questions. On the intranet being developed at JL, it would be useful to include Google as a feature because many people perform Google searches on a daily basis.

In looking at codified sources of information that JL staff access and apply to do their job, the JL databases and Web sites were used greatly on a daily basis (36 percent and 50 percent, respectively); however, JL staff actively apply their own database and personal contact list file (62 percent), as well as accessing their own notes or procedures (48 percent). This suggests that the existing databases and Web sites are not providing the full capability that staff members need, and it would be wise to include the staff "cheat sheets" as part of the intranet on how to get their jobs done.

Another interesting finding regarding knowledge resources is that JL, department, division, or vendor procedure manuals are rarely used. The JL policy manuals were used 39 percent on a monthly basis by staff members and 39 percent on a quarterly basis. Likewise, department- or division-specific procedure manuals or guidelines were never used by 44 percent of the respondents, and vendor-provided procedure manuals were never used 40 percent of the time.

In reviewing the list of hard-copy or Web-based resources that JL staff typically use to perform their job, those most often used on a daily basis were Google searches, Excel/Word forms developed internally, local and national newspaper Web sites, news clips from JL, and specialized financial Web sites. In developing the intranet, it would be useful to include these sites and resources for easy access and one-stop access.

For contacting outside experts, 78 percent of the time an outside peer, colleague, or expert is accessed for answers to questions on either a weekly or monthly basis. Everyone seems to have their own set of experts or outside colleagues, as the same names did not appear on a frequent basis from one staff member to the next. This suggests that each staff member has his or her own network of connections. It might be more effective to share these connections with other JL colleagues to build stronger ties with the "outside world."

Social network analysis can also be used on the knowledge audit responses to see how the employees are interacting with each other, based upon their length of service to JL. There are five communities of employees (those who have been at JL less than six months, those six months to less than one year, those one year to less than three years, those three years to less than five years, and those more than five years). A social network shows a healthy relationship in that the employees who are the newest in the organization are seeking advice to questions from those employees who are typically fairly senior (more than five years at JL). JL may want to consider a mentoring program or "buddy system" whereby those employees who have been working less than one year at JL can link up with those employees working one to three years at JL (currently, those working less than one year at JL are not generally seeking advice from their peers closest to their work experience at JL) to further build a sense of belonging in JL.

Knowledge Sharing and Use

The survey responses for knowledge use indicate that JL staff typically uses, in order: data or information one has to gather oneself from multiple sources and analyze/synthesize to answer a specific question (13 percent), recommendations one is asked to make based on data or information that one must find oneself (12 percent), and recommendations one is asked to make based on data or information that is given to him/her (11 percent). After a task has been completed in terms of a written document, JL staff members tend to save the document in an electronic file in one's personal directory (22 percent), save it on a shared directory (20 percent), and share/distribute it to others (19 percent). In addition, staff members will also save it in a personal paper file (17 percent).

When asked about sharing information or an announcement that may be useful to other JL staff, most respondents (57 percent) indicated that they would tell them about it or distribute a copy to them personally. These numbers indicate very encouraging news about displaying a knowledge-sharing culture at JL. For KM to work at JL, a knowledge-sharing culture is a key component for success (versus a knowledge-hoarding environment). Continuing to build and nurture this knowledge-sharing culture is tantamount for JL to meet its strategic goals. JL should consider including "learning and knowledge-sharing proficiencies" as part of the recognition and reward system in JL. Building trust is also a central part of knowledge sharing. From the social networks, most people seem to stay within their own department/division for seeking advice. This seems reasonable as most people are comfortable within the same working environment. One concern during this past year that has reduced the level of trust in JL is the constant restructuring of JL. JL should minimize the number of restructuring efforts to reduce employee fear. Let the current structure get stabilized for awhile so that people do not feel on edge about their existence in the organization. The respondents indicated that the main constraints to sharing were mainly availability of time, lack of a well-organized central internal repository (i.e., the intranet) that is regularly updated and accessed by all staff, knowledge of who has particular knowledge, and too many last-minute projects that shift priorities and work flow. The intranet should be developed to include a proper taxonomy for content and document management, and should also include a "yellow pages" locator of JL staff members and external experts. JL should also include a library, with library specialists, as part of JL. The library and associated specialists should be key team members of the intranet and KM group.

The responses emphasized the need for best practices and lessons learned as applied to JL internal and external activities. JL may want to consider a lessons-learned system (see NASA's lessons-learned information system at llis.nasa.gov) as part of its KM strategy. The lessons-learned system should include a push approach (versus a pull approach) to sending appropriate lessons to staff members at the time they need it.

In terms of critical knowledge at risk of being lost because of turnover or lack of backup expertise, there appear to be several potential gaps. Some of these include JL's institutional history (case studies from other regions), older grants, evaluation initiatives prior to the year 2000, relationship history with grantees, solutions to grant agreement disputes, etc. From the knowledge audit survey, it was unclear as to which areas are of the greatest concern. However, the follow-up interviews suggest that preserving and documenting the institutional knowledge of JL would greatly help those in the future to not reinvent the wheel.

Training/Tools and Knowledge Needs

Echoing the "personalization" theme that emanates throughout the survey respondents, most JL staff (24 percent) prefer to get formal face-to-face training outside the workplace to learn or improve a skill. Likewise, most staff members (24 percent) prefer to speak with a person in real time to help them do their job. Respondents indicated that they would like to have additional training in learning the "JL basics" and have online training modules that could be accessed easily as refreshers. A strong need to be better informed on company-wide activities was evident from the surveys. A calendar with all JL and related meetings (and deadlines) should be posted on the intranet, as well as summary reports. In terms of making knowledge available, survey respondents disagreed (23 percent) that there is no easy way to make their knowledge available to others in JL (38 percent had no opinion and 37 percent agreed). These numbers may suggest that people in JL feel they have knowledge that could help others in JL, but do not know the best mechanisms to share what they know with their colleagues. To address this concern, JL may want to think about including staff members' specialty/expertise areas in a "yellow pages" locator system on the intranet, having all-hands JL-wide tutorials, "hot topics" talks, and using the intranet for posting lessons learned and having online communities.

In terms of the information or knowledge that is currently needed to better perform in JL, many respondents discussed the need for better benchmarking data on other organizations' best practices, updated training on changing government regulations, systematic information on ongoing projects at JL, more comprehensive understanding of what everyone does at JL, and better understanding of customer needs. Through the development of the intranet and increased attention to communications flows within JL, many of these gaps will be filled. The intranet should also have access to JL PowerPoint slides, conference summaries, and other internal-related information.

Knowledge Flow

In terms of knowledge flow in the organization, respondents indicated how the knowledge flow in their area of responsibility could be improved. There were a myriad of responses, but several people converged on a number of key areas: (1) need to have a centralized online space for grant-making staff to find all relevant grant management policies, calendar, "how to" manuals, grant-making resources, etc.; (2) need to have more policy and research briefings for informed decision making and communications; (3) need more regular contact with staff in the regional offices; and (4) need more people-power to get work down to reduce overload. Much of the comments are centered on improved communications flow within and between groups. Cross-teams should help improve the communications flow in JL. Also, the intranet can serve as a central repository for posting meeting summaries, calendaring, locating internal and external experts, etc. Some respondents indicated that they felt hampered in trying to work with external partners. They felt knowledge sharing was hampered by JL's overbearing attitude toward ownership and credit, resulting in constraints in working with external partners more freely to disseminate knowledge. JL might want to examine its intellectual property policy to see whether it is too strongly worded.

When asked about the mission- or operation-critical knowledge that JL staff felt they possessed, there were many unique answers to this question. Everyone seemed to feel that they had a strong contribution to make in their area of expertise. The main recurring responses were best practices of high-performing organizations and policy development. Because several people have experience in knowing best practices to be used, the best-practice/lessons-learned system should tap the expertise of these individuals to include their best/worst practices in the system. Overall, from the additional comments provided in the survey, the staff members were pleased to participate in this knowledge audit study and felt it helped clarify their own role in JL.

Specific Key KM Recommendations for JL to Undertake

JL has been on its formal KM journey for the past two years, with its push to transform itself into a learning organization. Much of the early work in JL's KM strategy has focused on developing and sharing knowledge externally, building the technology infrastructure for this external knowledge sharing, developing codified repositories, and starting to educate the JL staff on KM principles. The first two years have been useful in terms of creating an awareness of KM throughout JL and leading the way in terms of reaching out to the external community for collaboration and exchanging knowledge and insights.

Now that the external focus is being supported, JL is now (appropriately) looking inwardly to best capture, share, and apply knowledge internally among its staff. As such, JL should consider a number of key initiatives as part of its KM strategy for this coming year:

Develop the Organizational Infrastructure to Support Knowledge Management in JL

This includes: having knowledge coordinators to help populate content in the intranet and Web portal, adding learning and knowledge-sharing proficiencies to the recognition and reward system at JL to emphasize and reward people for sharing knowledge, and embedding KM activities as part of everyone's daily work activities (e.g., capturing and using lessons learned/best practices during the project life cycle, having relevant "storytelling" for the first five to ten minutes of staff meetings, having after-action reviews at the end of each project, etc.). Processes should also be established for capturing knowledge such as having knowledge-elicitation sessions with a knowledge engineer, posting the weekly reports on the intranet and categorizing/indexing them by subject/topic area (versus strictly by date), writing down lessons learned on a weekly/monthly basis for sharing at staff meetings and posting on the intranet, exit interviews, etc.

Develop the Technology Infrastructure (i.e., Intranet) to Enable Knowledge Sharing to Take Place, as Well as Developing Quick-Win Pilot Projects

The intranet needs to be developed within JL, and appropriate resources should be allocated to ensure its development, content organization, nurturing, and maintenance. A calendar with all JL and related meetings (and deadlines) should be posted on the intranet, as well as having online modules and cheat sheets for JL training and how to perform various operations within JL. Lists of internal frequently asked questions and responses, synopses of JL and external reports, Excel/Word forms developed internally, local and national newspaper Web sites, and news clips from JL should also be included in the intranet. The Google search engine should be included as part of the intranet for both internal and Web searches. The intranet should also have links to two essential new projects: a "yellow pages" internal and external locator system and a lessons-learned/best-practices system. The yellow pages should also include organizational responsibilities and subject matter expertise. The lessons-learned system should also include a "push" feature to push appropriate new lessons to program staff and the external community who could benefit from these lessons. The yellow pages project should take priority over the lessons-learned system, and software such as AskMe (by AskMe Corporation) could be used to help create the yellow pages. A longer-term project that should be undertaken by JL is a Web-based, online-searchable knowledge preservation project to capture the institutional knowledge of expertise in JL and the rationale and decision-making process for why certain decisions were made. Additionally, a process and system to capture, analyze, interpret, and mine grant outcomes to inform JL strategies should also be established.

Accentuate the "Personalization" Approach to Knowledge Sharing within JL

A major part of this approach is to improve intercommunications flow between divisions. The communications division may want to develop a strategy to facilitate this flow and position themselves as central liaisons between the divisions. Cross teaming should also be encouraged, which will enable people-to-people networking and connections to be made outside of one's own community/division and integrate across functional silos. Posting of meeting summaries, conference/trip reports, PowerPoint slides, etc., should be put on the intranet. Knowledge-sharing forums between experienced staff and those who are newer to JL should be conducted, as well as having brown bag "learn and lunch" get-togethers. Because grants management is a core competency of JL, this may be a ripe area to target for such knowledge exchanges. A formal mentoring program should exist within JL, and this will also help in improving communications flow within JL, building and nurturing a knowledge-sharing culture, and increasing trust and a sense of belonging in JL. Additionally, improved communications flow needs to exist throughout JL, especially to the younger employees. Ways to make this improvement possible, besides a formal mentoring program, are: having "open" meetings (such as the quarterly update and adjust meetings, weekly team leads meetings, etc.) to keep everyone (especially the younger employees) better informed and capturing and posting the minutes/summaries of these key meetings on the intranet.

Instill a Stronger Feeling of Trust in JL by Minimizing the Number of Restructuring Efforts to Reduce Employee Fear and Improve Communications Flow within JL

Let the current structure get stabilized for some time so that people do not feel on edge about their existence in the organization. Additionally, by having JL create and follow a multiyear strategic plan (as what is now being done) versus the previous method of just an annual strategic plan, continuity in JL will be enhanced. Lastly, human capacity concerns have been echoed throughout the study, whereby people feel overworked, lack time to reflect, and often feel in a reactive mode versus proactive stance. Perhaps, business process and workload studies should be conducted to look at the health of JL in terms of improving work processes and reducing employee cognitive overloads.

If JL incorporates these recommendations toward developing its KM strategy and implementation plan, it will be on its way to successfully applying knowledge-sharing activities for transforming JL into a learning organization, enhancing its organizational intelligence, and improving communications and effectiveness internally and externally.

References

American Productivity and Quality Center, Carla O'Dell's Knowledge Management Presentation, *APQC Knowledge Management Conference*, Crystal City, VA, 2002.

Anderson, J., Evaluation in health informatics: social network analysis, *Computers in Biology and Medicine Journal*, Vol. 32, 2002.

Annie E. Casey Foundation, *Foundations Meeting on Knowledge Management, Proceedings* (also *Casey Newsletter*, July 1, 2003), Baltimore, MD, June 11, 2003a.

Annie E. Casey Foundation, Interview with Tom Kern, Knowledge Management Director, Baltimore, MD, July 21, 2003b.

Borgatti, S.P., Everett, M.G., and Freeman, L.C., *UCINET 6.0*, Natick, MA: Analytic Technologies. 2002.

Cravey, A., Washburn, S., Gesler, W., Arcury, T., and Skelly, A., Developing socio-spatial knowledge networks: a qualitative methodology for chronic disease prevention, *Social Science and Medicine Journal*, Vol. 52, 2001.

Cross, R., Borgatti, S., and Parker, A., Beyond answers: dimensions of the advice network, *Social Networks Journal*, Vol. 23, 2001.

Eldridge, D. and Wilson, E., Nurturing knowledge: the U.K. higher education links scheme, *Public Administration and Development Journal*, Vol. 23, 2003.

JL, personal interviews with key individuals in JL, conducted by Jay Liebowitz, July–August 2003.

Kleiner, A., Karen Stephenson's Quantum Theory of Trust, *Strategy+Business Magazine*, Booz Allen and Hamilton, Issue 29, 4th quarter, 2002.

Liebowitz, J., *Addressing the Human Capital Crisis in the Federal Government: A Knowledge Management Perspective*, Butterworth-Heinemann/Elsevier, Boston, MA, 2004.

Liebowitz, J., Montano, B., McCaw, D., Buchwalter, J., Browning, C., Newman, B., and Rebeck, K., The knowledge audit, *Journal of Knowledge and Process Management*, Vol. 7, No. 1, 2000.

Wexler, M., The who, what, and why of knowledge mapping, *Journal of Knowledge Management*, Vol. 5, 2001.

Chapter 4

Lessons Learned: The Intelligentsia Melting Pot

Business Intelligence Cannot Exist without Knowledge Management

Whether talking about business intelligence (BI) or competitive intelligence (CI), a key ingredient must exist — that is, knowledge management (KM). KM is determining how to best leverage knowledge internally and externally in an organization and how to create value out of the organization's intangible assets. Specifically, KM is the process of identifying, capturing, sharing, applying, disseminating, and creating knowledge in the organization's context.

As enterprise-wide BI implementations are a growing concern in the near term, KM has an important role in facilitating BI strategy formulation and implementation. As organizations are interested in applying BI best practices, KM also entails learning from previous success and failure. Lessons-learned systems (such as NASA's lessons-learned information system (LLIS) help in capturing, analyzing, and disseminating appropriate lessons to enable project teams and organizations strive for success. For example, NASA's LLIS includes over 1500 lessons in project management, safety, systems engineering, and other areas that benefit the NASA community.

Besides knowledge dissemination techniques, KM can enhance the BI process through its emphasis on knowledge elicitation and sharing techniques. Most people in the KM community classify knowledge as tacit and explicit, or fluid and sticky. *Tacit knowledge* is typically shared from people-to-people connections, whereas *explicit knowledge* is codified knowledge in the form of books, documents, memos, databases, etc. In the same way, fluid knowledge gets passed from one person to the next, and sticky knowledge is the knowledge that "sticks with you." To capture the "business rules" that drive the organization and a major part of the enterprise's BI, knowledge acquisition techniques from the KM field can help to elicit the business rules from those in the organization, as well as from the customers and stakeholders.

As BI and CI evolve, an understanding of the various links of entities and knowledge sources becomes important. The KM field has been applying social network analysis techniques to map the knowledge flows and detect knowledge gaps in the organization. Social network analysis has grown out of the anthropology and sociology disciplines, but can be of great assistance to mapping knowledge flows within the organization for enhancing BI methods. Discovery informatics (DI) can also be used to uncover patterns and relationships in large masses of data and text. Through the use of these knowledge discovery and data- or text-mining techniques, new patterns of information and knowledge can be inferred.

BI can also learn from the knowledge audit processes used in KM. A knowledge audit is similar to a manufacturing firm taking an inventory of its physical assets. Likewise, a knowledge audit takes an inventory of the organization's intellectual assets, including the human capital, structural capital, and social capital. By identifying knowledge sources, sinks, and flows in the organization as part of the knowledge audit, leverage points can be located that can help improve the BI processes of the firm.

Where Is the "Intelligence" behind "BI"?*

KM is a critical component of BI. Another discipline that should be a central ingredient of BI is artificial intelligence (AI) (and a subset of AI called DI). AI deals with supplementing human brain power with intelligent computer power, through the use of intelligent systems technologies such as knowledge-based systems, neural networks, intelligent agents, genetic algorithms, case-based reasoning, etc. DI is a subset of AI dealing

---

* Excerpts taken from J. Liebowitz's articles on www.businessintelligence.com (permission granted by Doug Campbell, Ed., May 23, 2005).

with discovering relationships and patterns in large masses of data and text. DI involves such technologies as data mining, text mining, rule induction, self-organizing maps, and other related techniques.

Much of what is being espoused about BI reminds one of the earlier conversations involving AI. Some people say that AI should have been called intelligence amplification (IA). In this sense, AI should have been designed to assist the human and support the decision maker versus trying to create a computer program to eventually replace the human. In the same way, there has not been much intelligence behind BI — BI techniques have been used to primarily support the decision maker.

Some organizations, such as CSIRO Australia (the Commonwealth Scientific and Industrial Research Organization), define BI to include five key stages: data sourcing, data analysis, situation analysis, risk assessment, and decision support. This definition takes on an AI flavor in terms of extracting, synthesizing, filtering, and discovering information from multiple sources of data. However, most people have not defined BI in the same manner. However, CSIRO has a refreshing view on BI that includes AI.

How could AI techniques help BI? Intelligent agents, for example, could be used in a number of ways to facilitate BI. They could be used to help "push" lessons learned and best practices to the decision maker via integration with lessons-learned systems. They could assist the BI user by developing a dynamic profile of the user's patterns and interests for better targeting information to the user. They could also be used as searching and filtering tools, as well as user profiling and classification aids. Expert systems technology could be applied to BI in utilizing knowledge elicitation techniques to acquire lessons learned. They could also be used as online pools of expertise in rule- or case-based systems. Through knowledge representation techniques used in the expert systems field, knowledge taxonomies and ontologies could also be better defined and developed for BI application.

Data mining and knowledge discovery techniques can help advance the BI field. For example, data- and text-mining methods can inductively determine relationships and rules for improved BI. They could also assist in generating new cases. Neural networks and genetic algorithms could enhance BI applications by helping to weed out rules and cases, looking for inconsistencies within knowledge repositories, and helping to filter noisy data.

Business rules and business rule engines, which can be partly derived from AI and BI techniques, are an excellent application of how AI has blended and synergized with BI. For example, on September 1, 2004, Fair Isaac Corporation, a leading provider of analytics and decision technology, and Lombardi Software, provider of business process management software, announced a partnership to provide organizations with an integrated solution incorporating Fair Isaac's Blaze Advisor business rules management software and Lombardi's TeamWorks business process management software. Fair Isaac Corporation, which has previously used neural networks in their products, has combined its business rules technology with business process management at the policy and decision-making levels of the organization. There is an active community of practitioners and researchers in business rules, as evidenced by the annual business rules conference.

Other conferences, such as the Knowledge Management and Business Intelligence workshop (KMBI, 2005) held in April 2005 in Germany, are promoting the integration of AI, KM, and BI. BI is being defined in this context as an active, model-based, and prospective approach to discover and explain hidden, decision-relevant aspects in large amounts of business data to better inform business decision processes.

BI needs to embed AI methods within its tool suite. According to Judith Lamont's article, "Competitive Intelligence (CI): Ingredients for Success" (*KMWorld*, 2002), she states that "many CI initiatives leave a big gap between information and action ... in addition, the corporate hierarchy does not always integrate CI into the top ranks." If BI does not incorporate such active components as AI and KM, BI may suffer the same fate as CI, as described by Lamont.

Perhaps, the problem is that there is too much "intelligence" around — AI, CI, BI, and other intelligentsia. Maybe it is time to package all these types of intelligence into one. We could call it "ABC Intelligence" to denote the basic building blocks (i.e., the ABCs) of nonhuman intelligence. Or, alternatively, the ABC Intelligence could refer to "artificial, business, and competitive" intelligence.

Improving Lessons-Learned Systems through Artificial Intelligence

Capturing and applying lessons learned are important processes in KM, systems engineering, and certainly in program/project management (Liebowitz, 1999, 2004; Liebowitz and Beckman, 1998). In NASA's terminology, a lesson learned is knowledge or understanding gained from experience. In this context, a lesson learned could be based upon a success or failure. NASA's LLIS has been in existence for about 11 years to help the NASA community learn from project management, systems engineering, and other types of lessons. Hopefully, these lessons learned avoid the repetition of past failures and mishaps, and enable the promulgation of best practices.

Besides NASA, the Department of Energy has been active in the lessons-learned area. The Society for Effective Lessons Learned Sharing (SELLS), through the U.S. Department of Energy, grew out of the formal Energy Department's lessons-learned program (http://www.eh.doe.gov/ll/sells/). The military, through after-action reviews, has been using lessons learned for many years. The U.S. Army, for example, through its Center for Army Lessons Learned (CALL) has been collecting lessons learned from combat missions for more than 20 years (http://call.army.mil/). Even private industry has been involved with lessons-learned systems, such as Xerox's Eureka system for exchanging tips among copier service repair persons.

Even though lessons-learned systems are developed to promote knowledge sharing, 70 percent of these systems are ineffective (Weber et al., 2001). A key reason for their ineffectiveness is due to the reliance on passive analysis and dissemination versus active approaches (Liebowitz, 1998; Liebowitz, 2001). Most lessons-learned systems use a "pull" approach to lesson analysis and dissemination whereby the users go to the lessons-learned Web site and perform a search to locate relevant lessons. As people are inherently busy, the task of going to yet another Web site is an additional burden on the user. A better approach would be to use a "push" approach, whereby relevant new lessons are sent to the user via an e-mail based on a completed user-interest profile. In fact, the NASA LLIS uses this approach as part of its over 1500 lessons-learned repository. The user completes a user-interest profile, and, as new lessons that fit the profile are entered into the LLIS, the user receives an e-mail with a URL link to quickly access that lesson.

The main problem with this approach is that it relies on a static profile of the user's interest. Thus, a lesson that was sent a few months ago may be needed now, and it is unlikely that the user will even remember the lesson that was previously sent.

Another problem with using lessons-learned systems deals with the process itself. For KM to be successful, KM practices must be embedded into the daily work activities of employees. For example, to encourage the submission and usage of lessons-learned, NASA requires every project team to capture lessons learned in a lessons-learned repository like the LLIS and be ready to show, during formal project reviews, the value-added benefits the team derived from accessing lessons learned. This requirement is part of the NPG7120.5B NASA program and project management processes and requirements. The Department of Energy has also tried to engrain lessons learned into everyday processes (Miller and Steinke, 2002).

Aside from the process issues, a major improvement in the use of lessons-learned systems is needed on the technology side in terms of providing a "push" approach for disseminating timely and relevant lessons to users. Such an approach will be highlighted in the following to allow more active lesson analysis and dissemination.

The NASA LLIS: A Case Study

To explain the "push" approach to lesson dissemination within a lessons-learned system, let us first look at a lessons-learned system to appreciate the context of using such an approach. The NASA LLIS, which grew out of a graduate student's thesis about 11 years ago, is the agency-wide official lessons-learned system. This Web-based system has been enhanced over the years, and has over 1500 lessons that relate to areas of interest to the NASA scientific, engineering, and management communities. Lessons are collected and verified from the ten NASA Centers and three associated sites. The general public can access lessons via the Public Lessons Learned System (PLLS), located at the http://llis.nasa.gov Web site. The welcome screen for the PLLS is shown in Figure 4.1.

A sample lesson from the PLLS, http://llis.nasa.gov/llis/plls/index.html, is displayed in Figure 4.2.

The NASA LLIS (not the PLLS) incorporates a user interest profiling feature, where the NASA user can mark the areas of interest for receiving new lessons submitted to the LLIS. This allows for a more proactive push approach for lesson dissemination. However, due to the static nature of the profile (unless the user constantly revises his or her profile), the user does not greatly benefit in terms of just-in-time lessons.

An improved method could apply intelligent agent and case-based reasoning. Through the use of intelligent agent technology and case-based reasoning (matching/adapting a new situation/case to previous situations/cases), the user can have a dynamic user profile built that in turn gets matched with the lessons in the lessons-learned system via case-based reasoning, as shown in Figure 4.3. An intelligent agent can be created to assist the user by developing a weekly profile based on e-mail received and sent by the user (with proper privacy provisions) and reviewing text documents. Already, software exists to develop this taxonomy and profile, such as Tacit's ActiveNet Application (www.tacit.com), by analyzing the user's existing enterprise systems such as document management, discussion databases, e-mail, instant messaging, and digital workspaces. Once the dynamic user interest profile is built on a weekly basis, case-based reasoning can be used to match this profile with new lessons entered in the lessons-learned system. In this manner, appropriate and timely lessons can be sent to the user, making the lessons-learned system a more effective part of KM.

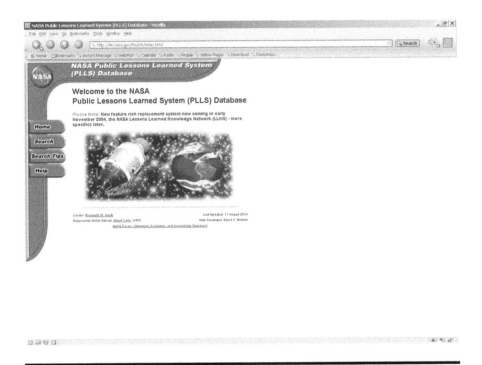

Figure 4.1   Welcome screen for the NASA public lessons-learned system.

Lessons Learned: CI and KM

Bob Galvin, the former Chairman of Motorola, spoke at the annual Society of Competitive Intelligence Professionals meeting in April 2005 about the five key traits of CI professionals. Motorola was one of the first companies to have a BI/CI unit. Galvin discussed the essential traits as: having an appreciation for anthropology, emphasizing human intelligence, being a good listener, being a creative thinker, and being counterintuitive (having something new to say). The ability to possess these characteristics will, at least in the eyes of Galvin, separate the successful CI professional from those who are not.

Galvin further discussed some of the lessons learned from his experience. One such lesson was "we win at the margin." This expression refers to decisions, and their successful impact, which typically result from having slightly more information or knowledge than those who do not. The difference is so fine that having a little more insight and knowledge can affect the successful outcome of a decision.

Additionally, as Galvin points out, senior management must promote the minority point of view. That is how advances and innovations are

PLLS Database Entry: 1479

Lesson Info

- **Lesson Number:** 1479
- **Lesson Date:** 02-apr-2004
- **Submitting Organization:** GSFC
- **Submitted by:** Scott Glubke

Subject/Title/Topic(s):

Lessons Learned from SNOE Reentry

Abstract:

The Student Nitric Oxide Explorer (SNOE) spacecraft and its instruments were designed and built at the Laboratory for Atmospheric and Space Physics (LASP) of the University of Colorado. SNOE was a small scientific satellite that measured the effects of energy from the sun and from the magnetosphere on the density of nitric oxide in the Earth's upper atmosphere. The SNOE was launched on February 27, 1998 and reentered on December 13, 2003 at 09:34 GMT.

This document summarizes the lessons learned for the reentry of the SNOE. Even though SNOE was a small spacecraft that had little possibility of impacting the earth, it was an excellent opportunity for SSMO to work through our perceived reentry process. These lessons learned will help to clarify the activities during the reentry of any other NASA mission. Also, recommendations for changes to the NASA Policy Directive (NPD 8710.3A), NASA Policy for Limiting Orbital Debris Generation, will also be suggested.

Predicting reentry dates is an important task for NASA to maintain public safety. Despite any minimal probability for debris impacting, the mission specific program/project must be aware of all reentry related information including launch vehicles and upper stages.
Summary of Lessons Learned:

Description of Driving Event:

Reentry of spacecraft into earth's atmosphere at end of life.

Lesson(s) Learned:

All of the lessons learned form the SNOE reentry are summarized below and are discussed in detail in the following section.

1. "Maintenance" of reentry information is not defined in the current version of NPD 8710.3A. Updates to the reentry information are done more on a "calendar" basis instead of a "relative reentry" basis.
2. The "coordination" of reentry information within the agency and "notification to appropriate personnel" is ambiguous within the NPD.
3. The "mission specific program/project" is responsible for implementing the orbital debris mitigation measures and guidelines. To be able to do this effectively the program needs to understand the orbit and reentry characteristics for each mission, and the daily operations and orbit determination activities are an essential input to the reentry predictions. The orbit determination activities are also necessary to plan the daily operational passes. Any "program specific" predictions must be coordinated with Code Q (OSMA).
4. CMOC routinely provides standard orbit data (TLE, etc) to GSFC OIG web site and to JSC. All NASA related reentry information is normally distributed to JSC. Any request for "special data" needs to be coordinated with CMOC and JSC so as not to cause confusion with the standard data processing.

Figure 4.2   Sample lesson from the NASA public lessons-learned system.

Recommendation(s):

There are three areas that should be addressed in the NPD. The fourth recommendation is for GSFC information and does not impact the NPD and is not discussed here.

First, a better definition of what is required to "maintain" the reentry information should be developed. Several different viewpoints exist as to how often the predictions should be updated. GSFC has developed a set of revised guidelines that should be incorporated into the NPD or used as a starting point for further discussion.

Secondly, clarification of who is "appropriate personnel" is required. There were several instances during the SNOE reentry where some people had received updated information while others had not. A clear distribution list of "appropriate" offices should be defined.

Finally, the "mission specific program/project" has a definite responsibility and participation in the reentry activities. The program office (SSMO) must be able to effectively manage the daily operations and the EOM plan. Consistent and timely updates to the reentry predictions are necessary for budget and manpower planning. Any mission specific reentry predictions must be coordinated with Code Q. At some point the mission specific predictions should transition to the CMOC predictions via the ODPO. A possible transition point could be reentry minus 30 days.

Evidence of Recurrence Control Effectiveness:

N/A

Documents Related to Lesson:

NPD 8710.3A, NASA Policy for Limiting Orbital Debris Generation

Applicable NASA Enterprise(s):

- Space Science

Applicable Crosscutting Process(es):

N/A

Additional Key Phrase(s):

- Disposal
- Flight Operations
- Policy & Planning
- Safety & Mission Assurance
- Spacecraft

Approval Info:

- **Approval Date:** 18-jun-2004
- **Approval Name:** XXX
- **Approval Organization:** GSFC
- **Approval Phone Number:** XXX-XXX-XXXX

Figure 4.2 Sample lesson from the NASA public lessons-learned system (continued).

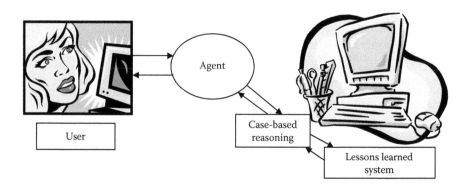

Figure 4.3 Turning the lessons-learned process from passive to active.

made. Before making a decision, a manager should always consider the minority report, similar to doing a SWOT (strengths-weaknesses-opportunities-threats) analysis. The CI professional can provide this counterintuitive, out-of-the-box thinking so that minority opinions can be formulated, as well as the majority views.

Another interesting lesson learned about CI is that much more time is spent in the collection function versus the analysis activity of the CI professional. According to Jonathan Calof, from the University of Ottawa (SCIP Conference, April 2005), about 50 percent or more of the CI professional's time is spent on collection. A more desirable target may be 25 percent, and the CI professional is not spending enough time on the analysis function. Scenario planning, profiling, competitor audits, war gaming, simulations, data mining, and other techniques should be applied by the CI professional in doing the analysis function.

James Bruce, with the U.S. government, echoes the need for improved analysis on the part of CI professionals. In his talk, "Analysis and Process: Lessons Learned from US Government Intelligence Experience," (SCIP Conference, April 7, 2005), he discusses eight cases and in all eight cases, better analysis would have helped (and was possible). He expresses the need to have alternative interpretations of available information, alternative scenarios for different outcomes, and alternative (competing) hypotheses for making better decisions. Bruce feels that challenging assumptions is vital, applying better analytical imagination, and using "alternative analysis" (such as analysis of competing hypotheses, devil's advocacy, and alternative scenarios) are important analysis lessons learned for the CI professional. This translates well to the business world by providing the value-added dimension: namely, posing the right questions, understanding the company's information needs and information priorities, driving the collection process, providing interpretations of complex data and early warnings, and improving the decision maker's basis for action. Bruce further identifies the key lessons from the government with respect to intelligence: "good" information matters; intelligence, especially analysis, can provide a decisive information advantage; good analysis requires good collection (human intelligence is especially important); and professionalism is a must.

CI is similar to looking out your office window, and KM is like looking down your office hallway. With KM, you are typically looking for human capital and knowledge flows within the organization. With CI, you are primarily gazing out and doing an environmental scan to keep track of the competition. Whether CI or KM, a key lesson learned is to align your CI or KM strategy with your organization's strategic goals.

Another key lesson learned from KM implementations that will help organizations make better informed decisions is the three high-level tenets of collaborative business knowledge, as discussed by Jonathan Spira ("Time to (Re)Innovate the Office?", *KMWorld*, June 2005):

- *The one-environment rule:* Being in one environment for all tasks
- *Friction-free knowledge sharing:* Easily sharing information without having to think about it
- *Embedded community:* Being able to communicate and collaborate contextually

Organizations can add strategic value by overcoming CI blind spots. According to Jody Holtzman of AARP ("Adding Strategic Value by Overcoming CI Blind Spots," SCIP Conference, April 2005), a single goal of organizations is typically: to inform and strengthen the company's strategies, operations, and most importantly decision making, and thereby help attain sustained competitive advantage. Holtzman feels that the cause of intelligence failure is not what is seen, but what is not seen (i.e., blind spots). There could be five types of CI blindspots, as identified by Holtzman:

- *Behavioral and psychological blind spots:* Blinded by biases
- *Internal blind spots:* Caused by potential ignorance of the company's strengths and weaknesses
- *Big picture blind spots:* Caused by organizational silos
- *Philosophical blind spots:* Consciously imposed constraints on the CI manager, such as internal politics
- *Opportunity blind spots:* Not understanding how to define and scope a business opportunity

Holtzman feels that organizations, and in particular, CI analysts, can surmount these CI blind spots by testing assumptions, looking at the competition within a dynamic integrated market context, knowing your own strengths and weaknesses (as well as those of your competitors), moving beyond early warning risk management, and examining the "so what" and "what if" of business implications.

Joe Goldberg, Director of BI for Motorola Inc. ("From So-What to What to Do?", SCIP Conference, April 2005), indicates that the global BI cycle should: (1) identify key intelligence topics, (2) create the knowledge base, (3) collect intelligence, (4) make the intelligence actionable and available, and (5) provide action for businesses and intelligence users. Goldberg indicates that sometimes we drop the ball when providing intelligence, such as selecting a "good enough" answer, focusing on a narrow range of alternatives, concentrating on the "most politically correct" solution, or even ignoring the intelligence. The goal of the CI analyst should be to move from a tactical focus to a strategic one to provide an actionable recommendation based upon expertise and analysis of the issue. As Goldberg describes, integrate your CI with strategy, and worry about things that are relevant.

Summary

Lessons learned abound over the years from the use of KM, BI, and CI. The synergy between these three areas and the resulting best practices contribute to the formulation of "strategic intelligence" — that is, improving the organization's strategic decision-making capabilities. KM, BI, and CI can provide value-added benefits toward increasing the strategic intelligence of the organization. This chapter highlighted some quick takeaways to help organizations improve in these areas.

References

Liebowitz, J., *Addressing the Human Capital Crisis in the Federal Government: A Knowledge Management Perspective*, Butterworth-Heinemann/Elsevier, Burlington, MA, 2004.

Liebowitz, J., *Knowledge Management: Learning from Knowledge Engineering*, CRC Press, Boca Raton, FL, 2001.

Liebowitz, J. (Ed.), *The Knowledge Management Handbook*, CRC Press, Boca Raton, FL, 1999.

Liebowitz, J. (Ed.), *The Handbook on Applied Expert Systems*, CRC Press, Boca Raton, FL, 1998.

Liebowitz, J. and Beckman, T., *Knowledge Organizations: What Every Manager Should Know*, CRC Press, Boca Raton, FL, 1998.

Miller, C. and Steinke, W., Building a Better Lessons Learned Program, Idaho National Engineering and Environmental Laboratory, Report INEEEL/EXT-02-00426, Idaho Falls, ID, 2002.

Weber, R., Aha, D., and Becerra-Fernandez, I., Intelligent lessons learned systems, *Expert Systems with Applications: An International Journal* (Liebowitz, J., Ed.), Vol. 20, No. 1, 2001.

Chapter 5

Competitive Intelligence

Introduction

When some people hear the term *competitive intelligence* (CI), they often think of industrial espionage or spying. Even though the term may imply some overtones of these activities, CI is really involved with developing a systematic program for capturing, analyzing, and managing external (and internal) information and knowledge to improve the organization's decision-making capabilities. CI's focus is more on external views, but some people feel that it could include internal perspectives as well.

Knowledge management (KM) and business intelligence (BI) are closely linked with CI. KM deals with how best to leverage knowledge internally within the organization and externally to the organization's customers and stakeholders. Certainly, some cultures are more permissive and receptive to knowledge sharing. For example, in Jonathan Calof's study at the University of Ottawa (performed for the Society of Competitive Intelligence Professionals), Canada was more open toward knowledge sharing versus the United Kingdom and France. This influences how willing people are toward sharing their information and knowledge. Similarly, BI deals with how best to capture and share internal information to make it widely available throughout the organization. KM and BI are close cousins to CI.

CI is similar, in a way, to playing sports. Scouting out your opponents helps you to prepare a game plan in advance. For example, as a tennis player, you may know, through learning from others, that your opponent has a weak backhand and is a little slow of foot on the court. This CI helps you to develop a winning strategy by keeping most of the shots to your opponent's backhand and running him all over the court. Other external conditions factor into account. For example, if it is a windy day, then you may undercut the tennis ball when going against the wind, as the wind will slow the ball into drop shots. By using the wind, you can take advantage of the environmental conditions by outsmarting your opponent. Of course, planning and execution are two different things. You may have a good strategy and plan based on your CI, but if you do not execute it well or adapt from it, if your strategy is not working, then you probably will not be successful.

CI is as simple as that — collect, analyze, develop, and manage; collect the appropriate information and knowledge, analyze the information and knowledge, develop an approach based on the synthesis of the results, and manage your expectations and strategy, and adjust accordingly.

What Not to Do in CI

Bill Fiora, with Outward Insights, discusses the "7 Deadly Sins of CI" ("The Seven Deadly Sins of CI," SCIP Conference, April 2005). Fiora points out the following:

- Most CI professionals are not aggressive enough in their jobs. Fiora advises taking a creative and entrepreneurial approach to CI by building personal networks to collect primary source intelligence and marketing CI within their organizations.
- This leads to the second sin being the failure to market the CI function. Successful CI teams use an organized marketing plan that includes road-show presentations around the organization, presentations to management on recent intelligence successes and return on investment, and intelligence products that are unique to CI.
- The third sin is neglecting early warning. Successful CI teams have an organized and systematic early warning process. Early warning must balance management's key intelligence topics (KITs) and the CI team's own list of early warning topics.
- The fourth sin is substituting synthesis for analysis. Fiora indicates that many times, CI practitioners perform 90 percent of the work on an intelligence project, but stop one step short of delivering true actionable analysis. For analysis to be actionable, it should be forward looking and decision relevant. Actionable intelligence is created, not collected. Furthermore, distilling 100 pages of information into 2 pages is synthesis, not analysis. Fiora defines *actionable analysis* as an assessment of how these changes will affect

the competitor's future strategy, obstacles it will face in implementing this strategy, and areas in which this strategy may conflict with your own company's objectives.

■ The fifth sin, according to Fiora, is using analytic tools as a substitute for creative thinking. Different analytic tools like SWOT (strengths-weaknesses-opportunities-threats) analysis, Michael Porter's Five Forces, or Value Chain Analysis are not sufficient as a replacement for creative thinking. They help provide a decision-making construct, but you need your own brains in interpreting the results and how they can apply toward improving organizational decisions.

■ The sixth major sin of CI is using only published information sources. Forward-looking analysis is typically collected from people (internal and external company sources, key opinion leaders, trade shows and conferences, journalists, consultants, industry observers, and others).

■ The last major sin is buying software too soon. You need to determine the best way for intelligence to function in your organization and then select the software packages that best support this capability.

Ben Gilad, of the Fuld Gilad Herring Academy of Competitive Intelligence, and Wayne Rosenkrans, of AstraZeneca, focus on the role of CI in strategy. In their presentation, "The Role of CI in Strategy" at the SCIP April 2005 Annual Conference, they indicate that typical CI professionals spend 80 percent of their time engaged in operational improvement tasks, and only 20 percent of the time playing a role in strategy. CI and strategic position are closely related, whether finding opportunities to strengthen position or identifying risks to uniqueness, as Gilad and Rosenkrans point out. Maybe 80 percent of the time should be spent on playing a role in strategy versus simply operational improvements. They suggest a new model to strategy development that follows the cycle shown in Figure 5.1.

Business strategy and issues →
Strategy formulation →
Strategy articulation →
Strategy execution →
Intelligence collection →
Implication analysis → Loops back to business strategy & issues
and strategy formulation

Figure 5.1 Cycle for new model to strategy development.

The CI Life Cycle

The CI life cycle, called *CSAS* (do not try to pronounce this acronym in front of your boss), can be thought of as shown in Figure 5.1. CI collection is one of the important first steps in performing CI. Typically, the collection of primary and secondary source information is performed by the CI professional. A primary source is getting information or knowledge directly from that source, either an individual, dataset, or document. Interviewing people or meeting individuals at tradeshows or conferences could provide some primary-source intelligence. A secondary source is getting information from a "once-removed" source of intelligence — in other words, a person who knows the individual who has the information, or a secondary source could be a newspaper article, industry report, or someone quoting someone else.

The synthesize stage is taking the collected information and distilling it into manageable snip-its and executive summaries. Some people confuse this phase with analyze. Analysis is more proactive and forward thinking. Scenario planning, SWOT analysis, balanced scorecard, and other techniques can be used as analytical aids to help make sense out of the synthesized information. Advanced knowledge discovery techniques, such as data and text mining, can reveal hidden patterns and relationships in large volumes of data and unstructured text. The goal of the analyze phase is to produce actionable intelligence to inform organizational decision making, which leads into the strategize step. An organization's business strategy, both short-term and long-term, can be influenced by the analyzed CI, which can alter or affect an organization's strategy. As the strategy unfolds, there will be new requirements for collecting information to support, refine, or modify the organization's strategy, and the CI cycle starts all over.

Linking CI with Strategic Intelligence

From the previous discussion and the CI life cycle, the link between CI and strategy becomes obvious. In formulating a strategy, CI is an important ingredient toward developing, monitoring, and adapting the strategy based on internal and external factors. With the merging of CI, KM, and BI, strategic intelligence (SI) becomes enabled as the strategic functions of the organization can be better informed for improving the decision-making process. SI, through leveraging the internal and external intelligence from KM, BI, and CI, is created to help the organization maximize its strategic mission and vision.

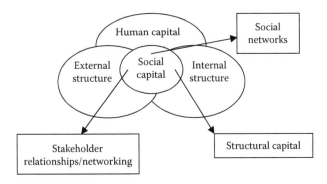

Figure 5.2   Social capital and market performance model (Lawrence Lock Lee, Computer Sciences Corporation, IC Congress 05).

Let us take an example of how this can work to generate SI. One organization was trying to boost employee morale and satisfaction through a variety of means, ranging from human resources incentives to technical solutions. An employee survey was conducted and analyzed through a BI approach — use of a database and data warehouse. KM principles were applied to show that recognition and reward structures needed to be put in place to encourage and nurture a knowledge-sharing culture. CI was used to see how other divisions, both within the organization under study as well as other organizations in the industry, were improving employee satisfaction and morale in their respective organizations.

The combination of the KM, BI, and CI provided enough SI to allow the organization to change the way it was growing and rewarding its human capital. The heart of an organization is its people, and if the employees are not happy, then the organization will be working suboptimally. Employee morale is a key strategic issue for any organization, and any CEO will tell you that the organization's competitive edge is its people. Thus, the coupling of KM, BI, and CI approaches helped to provide the necessary SI to improve employee morale and ultimately help the organization achieve its strategic mission and goals.

Another way to link CI, KM, and BI is through Lawrence Lock Lee's model of social capital, as shown in Figure 5.2.

In discussing the effect of social capital and market performance, Lawrence Lee (from Computer Sciences Corporation, Australia; introduced the model at the Intellectual Capital Congress 05) presents a model to show how social capital is comprised of human capital, internal, and external structures. Human capital promotes the social networks and knowledge flows within the organization. The external structure, through networking and stakeholder relationships, contributes to an organization's social capital. The internal structure, through the organization's structural capital (i.e., things you can't easily take home with you from the office, such as intellectual property rights, certain databases, etc.), enhances the organization's social capital.

What Do I Need to Be Trained or Educated in CI?

A number of universities are offering certificate or degree programs in CI through their business schools, library and information science schools, and others. For example, Drexel University offers a three-course certificate in CI. Simmons College in Boston has been offering a CI program over the past few years. The University of Ottawa, Brigham Young University, University of Pittsburgh, and several other universities have courses in CI. Johns Hopkins University, through its Graduate Division of Business and Management, launched a Graduate Certificate in CI in January 2005. The focus of the Johns Hopkins University program is more on the "analysis" and "informed decision making" functions as related to CI, see Figure 5.3. For example, the Hopkins CI Certificate consists of the following five courses:

1. Competitive intelligence
2. Knowledge management systems
3. Data mining and discovery informatics
4. Organizational and legal issues in technology
5. Information security foundations

Those in the MBA program at Johns Hopkins University can also concentrate on CI by taking the first four courses listed in the preceding text.

Besides universities, companies, professional societies, and special institutes offer education programs in CI. The Society of CI Professionals (SCIP — www.scip.org) offers many CI courses as part of their CI professional society. The Fuld Gilad Herring Academy of Competitive Intelligence also gives CI courses throughout the world. Many companies, such as Motorola, have in-house CI training courses.

CI techniques and tools should be part of every decision maker's toolkit for informed and improved decision making. Many people enter the CI field from marketing, product development, business development, strategy, information technology, information security, information and library sciences, and other domains. The key point is that irrespective of the background of the individual, CI is a necessary component toward making good decisions. Without knowing your competition or key factors that may affect your industry in the near and long term, how could anyone

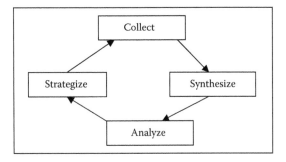

Figure 5.3   CI life cycle.

make a comfortable decision? The external and internal factors are important criteria that affect the development and outcome of a decision.

Whether dealing with CI, BI, or KM, the issue of "knowledge is power" becomes an important point of discussion. In the KM world, we prefer to use the adage "sharing knowledge is power." In KM, we strive to leverage knowledge in an organization through the sharing of others. In BI and CI, there may also be a "sharing knowledge is power" attitude as you speak with others, for example, to better explore what the competition is doing. However, CI can also portray a "knowledge is power" phenomenon as you probably want to be closed-lipped outside your organization in terms of competitive spirits.

In pushing a "sharing knowledge is power" discipline, organizations need to look at their recognition and reward systems to see how their employees may be motivated to share what they know. The following section looks at the best practices in this area.

Best Practices and Research Relating to Recognition and Reward Systems for Knowledge Sharing*

Sue Hanley, formerly the director of the collaboration/portal practice at Dell (Bethesda, Maryland), indicated in the Knowledge Management in Government Annual Conference (May 2005) that incentives and rewards must be matched to the organization's culture. She spoke of considering team-based rather than individual incentives, reward content creation as well as reuse, and champion knowledge-sharing behavior as well as portal usage to facilitate culture change.

---

* Per Jay Liebowitz's report for Tom Kern at the Annie E. Casey Foundation, Baltimore, MD, May 2005.

In the American Productivity and Quality Center's (APQC, Houston, Texas) 20-member organization study on "Rewards and Recognition in Knowledge Management" (July 2002), the key point made is to examine the rewards and recognition structure to ensure that knowledge-sharing principles and behaviors are aligned. Recognition, in this sense, is visible public reinforcement to individuals and teams for contributions and role modeling of behavior. Rewards such as money, promotions, and substantial gifts are more tangible.

According to Carla O'Dell, the president of APQC and a KM advocate, intrinsic motivation originates internally and emerges when the task itself seems rewarding and meets a person's goals. Extrinsic motivation originates externally and can cause the task to be perceived as a means to a rewarding end. The research shows that if you increase extrinsic motivation, you can drive out intrinsic reward. The goal is to foster intrinsic motivation, which is more permanent and lasting, versus the temporary extrinsic motivation.

For example, Jeanne Holm, who is the chief knowledge architect at the NASA Jet Propulsion Laboratory, indicated that 60 percent of the folks who were mentoring were doing it because of intrinsic rewards — they thought it was the right thing to do, and they got internal satisfaction from doing it.

According to the APQC study, extrinsic rewards become a detriment when:

- An organization attributes more importance to money than it actually has.
- Money is more prominent than it needs to be.
- Compensation is confused with rewards.
- Competition for rewards negatively impacts teamwork.
- Employees conceal problems to gain rewards.
- Rewards ignore the underlying issues behind behaviors.

Carla O'Dell indicates four rules of thumb for fostering a knowledge-sharing culture:

1. Always acknowledge the contributor of ideas.
2. Provide special recognition to volunteers, change agents, and role models (those people who take their personal time and devote energy to contribute or lead a KM effort or community).
3. Subject matter experts are usually intrinsically motivated and value the opportunity to increase their own professional development.
4. Create safe places to share.

Siemens AG rewards top-quality contributors to their ShareNet system with professional development opportunities such as attending/presenting at a global knowledge-sharing conference and earning ShareNet points that can be redeemed for goods.

A key lesson learned is to recognize both parties or units involved, including those who share knowledge and those who use knowledge. American Management Systems used their "Best Knews" newsletter to indicate the names of the individuals whose lessons learned/best practices in AMS' Lotus Notes KM system were accessed the most in the given month. Another important lesson, and perhaps the most important one, is that the recognition and reward system must be aligned with the organizational culture.

Prabhu Guptara (director, Organizational and Executive Development Center, UBS A.G., Ermatingen, Switzerland) feels that an organization's recognition and reward is an important component for encouraging knowledge-sharing activities (http://growth-strategies.com/subpages/businesswritings/015.html). One approach used by some companies is to take a "top slice" off the overall bonus pool available to a division and use it for the "best" cross-product contribution. This may help toward having a relationship-building culture versus a power-building one.

In Larry Stevens' article, "Incentives for Sharing" (*Knowledge Management Magazine*, October 2000), he discusses the range of recognition and reward programs used for instilling a knowledge-sharing culture. They range from kudos in the company newsletter to substantial pay bonuses. Several approaches could be considered. One approach used by Collective Technologies, an E-business consulting firm in Austin, Texas, is "hire people who will share." Collective Technologies evaluates all employees on criteria that include how many posted questions they have answered, how quickly they answered them, and when they got an acceptable answer, and how often they summarized the question and answer and posted them to the company network.

Another approach is to build trust, such as that used by Buckman Laboratories. Building a code of ethics is a first step in trust-building. Cap Gemini Ernst & Young believes that organizations must vary motivations depending on the level of the employee. For example, employees who publish research papers or post information to company discussion groups or chat rooms receive royalty points when others use that information. These points can be applied for a number of privileges, including extra vacation time. Additionally, knowledge sharing is part of their employee appraisals. Employees cannot earn the higher numbers unless they have actively participated and contributed to knowledge-sharing activities.

Harris Government Communications Systems believes in the "show public recognition" approach. They have a "Wall of Fame" in the main lobby, and it contains plaques with the names of employees who have excelled at knowledge sharing. Northrop Grumman Air Combat Systems uses the "reorganize for sharing" approach. Through the use of integrated product teams, knowledge sharing becomes more commonplace.

In the McKinsey Nonprofit Practice report, "Building Knowledge Management Capabilities" (August 2001), McKinsey identifies incentives as a key driver of effective knowledge creation. They indicate the need to establish minimum standards for expected contribution, offer rewards or recognition for outstanding efforts, and provide quick, easy access to submitted knowledge as a tangible result of efforts. In the *McKinsey Quarterly* article, "Creating a Knowledge Culture" (Hauschild et al., 2001), more than 70 percent of the successful companies surveyed, for example, had individual incentive systems linked to product development targets, compared with 27 percent of the less successful companies. McKinsey believes strongly in tying incentives to goals that employees can influence but not achieve on their own (which forces them to seek and offer knowledge more broadly).

The ability to share knowledge for increasing innovation, customer satisfaction, knowledge retention, and sense of community can be facilitated by a proper recognition and reward structure. In a sense, organizations such as Casey should strive to build "reflective practitioners" to promote a continuous learning culture. This will then allow for individual transformation to hopefully metamorphose into organizational transformation for developing a true "knowledge organization." At Marriott, the fundamental value is "take good care of your associates and they will take good care of your customers, and your customers will come back." The CEO Bill Marriott has a training philosophy "train to retain." According to Accenture's April 2005 report, "People, Performance, and Profit: Maximizing Human Capital" (Montgomery Research, Inc., San Francisco, California), George Hall (senior vice president of information resources–human resources) indicates the importance of recognizing the work of their people. For example, Marriott has a company-wide J. Willard Marriott Sr. Award of Excellence for honoring associates for consistently exceeding expectations, leading by example, and enhancing the lives of their co-workers. Managers are also encouraged to reward associates with team dinners and celebrations, cash bonuses, outings, and recognition in group events.

IBM, through Michael Bazigos' talk on "Asset Innovation and Transformation at IBM" at the Navy Annual Workforce Development and Research Conference (April 2005, Crystal City, Virginia), has a "Workforce Management Initiative" underway. According to Bazigos (director of global learning partnerships at IBM), this initiative is a series of strategies, policies, processes, and tools that enable optimal labor deployment built on a foundation of learning. The workforce requirements for IBM are: place a premium on collaboration and innovation, build deep industry expertise, develop deep process knowledge and service capabilities, achieve productivity through innovative workforce models, and place an ongoing focus on development.

Caterpillar, Inc., found that their employees were willing to contribute their knowledge to virtual knowledge-sharing communities of practice because the employees viewed their knowledge as a public good, belonging not to them individually, but to the whole organization (see Alexander Ardichvili et al., "Motivation and Barriers to Participation in Virtual Knowledge-Sharing Communities of Practice," *Journal of Knowledge Management*, Vol. 7, No. 1, 2003). Other reasons identified for contributing knowledge at Caterpillar's online communities were that employees felt the need to establish themselves as experts, and people felt it was important to "give back" to the organization.

According to the APQC Study on "Developing Rewards and Recognition for Knowledge Sharing" (September 2001), Hewlett-Packard Consulting has a Knowledge Masters Award to recognize employees whose knowledge mastery best exhibits the culture of balancing innovation with reuse and contributes to significant and measurable business impact.

In a research study, Gee-Woo Bock et al. (2005) recently published a paper in the *MIS Quarterly*, the leading information systems research journal, "Behavioral Intention Formation in Knowledge Sharing," (*MIS Quarterly*, Vol. 29, No. 1, March 2005). In a field survey of 154 managers from 27 Korean organizations, they made the following findings:

■ A felt need for extrinsic rewards may very well hinder, rather than promote, the development of favorable attitudes toward knowledge sharing (i.e., do not stress extrinsic rewards as a primary motivator for knowledge-sharing activities).

■ An organizational climate conducive to knowledge sharing exerts a strong influence on the formation of subjective norms regarding knowledge sharing.

■ An individual's attitude toward knowledge sharing is driven primarily by anticipated reciprocal relationships regarding knowledge sharing.

■ An individual's sense of self-worth through knowledge sharing intensifies the salience of the subjective norm regarding knowledge sharing.

Molly McLure-Wasko and Samer Farag, in their recent *MIS Quarterly* (March 2005, Vol. 29, No.1) article, "Why Should I Share?," found in their research that people contribute their knowledge when they perceive that it enhances their professional reputations, when they have the experience to share, and when they are structurally embedded in the network.

In Soonhee Kim and Hyangsoo Lee's research titled "Organizational Factors Affecting Knowledge Sharing Capabilities in E-Government: An Empirical Study" (*Knowledge Management in Electronic Government*, Maria Wimmer (Ed.), Springer-Verlag, 2004), they found that those public organizations with a high degree of social networks and a high degree of reward systems produced a high degree of knowledge-sharing capabilities.

Ashley Bush and Amrit Tiwana's article, "Designing Sticky Knowledge Networks" (*Communications of the ACM*, May 2005), discusses a four-year study of 122 users of four successful knowledge networks. They found that the features of the system that manage users' perceptions of their personal reputations and relationships with their peer users within the knowledge network increase stickiness (i.e., the user's desire to continue using a knowledge network system). Additionally, in Mohammed Quaddus and Jun Xu's article, "Adoption and Diffusion of Knowledge Management Systems: Field Studies of Factors and Variables" (*Knowledge-Based Systems Journal*, Vo. 18, 2005), they found that the major variables affecting KM system diffusion are organizational culture, top management support, and benefits to individuals.

In Howard Risher's November 2004 study, "Pay for Performance: A Guide for Federal Managers," sponsored by the IBM Center for the Business of Government, the main theme is that a new reward system needs to be put in place for the U.S. government (In fact, the Department of Defense and Department of Homeland Security will be implementing new pay systems.). Several principles relating to reward management are emphasized in Risher's study:

- When rewards are linked to specific results, it sends a powerful message relating to management's priorities.
- The "rules" for earning awards need to be transparent and managed consistently (in agreement with expectancy and equity theories).
- The receipt of an award should follow the accomplishment in a timely manner (consistent with reinforcement theory).
- When special projects and crises require unexpected attention, and an employee has to put in extra time or defer normal work duties, it may be that the unexpected work effort justifies special recognition, time off, or a tangible award.
- Employees are naturally looking for fairness and equity and are therefore interested in information relating to award recipients and the amount of awards.

In Terence O'Hara's article, "Study of Fannie Mae Cites Perverse Executive-Pay Policy" (*The Washington Post*, March 31, 2005), Fannie Mae's practice of awarding cash bonuses based on growth in earnings per share provided incentives for senior managers to manipulate accounting in Fannie Mae's huge portfolio of mortgage investments to reach earnings targets. Fannie Mae, with the recent troubles, eliminated all bonus programs based on earnings-per-share growth as of March 2005.

The Public Service Commission in Canada has "knowledge, information, and data should be shared" as one of its four guiding principles (see Jay Liebowitz and Yan Chen (2003), "Knowledge Sharing Proficiencies: The Key to Knowledge Management," *The Handbook on Knowledge Management* (Vol. 1, C. Holsapple, Ed., Springer-Verlag)). They indicate:

- Sharing will be rewarded.
- Performance evaluations should be linked to how well a person contributes to generating, assessing, and transferring knowledge.
- Knowledge will be available to all employees except where there is a demonstrated need for confidentiality or protection of privacy.
- Our knowledge will be shared to support collaboration with other federal government departments, other levels of government, and our other partners.
- We will establish processes and tools to enable us to capture and share our knowledge to support collaboration.

The World Bank has learning and knowledge-sharing proficiencies as part of its annual employee performance evaluation. These factors are: open to new ideas and continuous learning; shares own knowledge, learns from others, and applies knowledge in daily work; builds partnerships for learning and knowledge sharing. Similarly, Chevron has metrics around sharing and reuse as part of the annual performance evaluation, technical career ladders, promotion, and job-posting processes.

As discussed in this background research of organizational best practices for recognition and reward systems to encourage knowledge sharing, a fair amount of work has been studied and applied in this area. From a 20-organization benchmarking study in the development and use of recognition and reward systems for knowledge sharing (sponsored by APQC, "Developing Rewards and Recognition for Knowledge Sharing," December 2001), the following general principles have been suggested:

- Time to use and create knowledge has to be recognized and rewarded; if participants feel that they have to "steal" time from the "real" work to do this, they will not.

- Using the knowledge system has to be self-rewarding to the consumer; users have to get something out of it, be it knowledge they need or a sense of status and recognition.
- Recognition lies in being perceived as an expert by employees and management. Ensure that an internal expert's name is attached to documents, guidelines, and presentations they created.
- Create recognition for sharing, transferring, and using knowledge and best practices; you can do that by celebrating best practice success stories and propagating tales of big savings and important contributions.
- Recognize all parties or units involved, both those who share knowledge and those who receive knowledge; if both ends are not feeling rewarded, you will not get the results desired.
- A standardized reward system may help institutionalize the practice into the common culture.

Other examples from best-practice organizations indicate to host visible knowledge-sharing events and embed sharing knowledge into "routine" work processes.

Summary

This chapter provided some background on CI and how CI can play a role in SI. Similarly, how best to encourage a knowledge-sharing environment, particularly with emphasis on an organization's recognition and reward structure, was discussed in this chapter. By now, it should become apparent that KM, BI, and CI are closely linked and form the synthesis for SI. The next chapter will look at SI and how organizations can improve their strategic decision making.

Chapter 6

Strategic Intelligence: The Core of Executive Decision Making

Introduction

When people first hear the term *strategic intelligence* (SI), they think of military or defense intelligence. Even though the roots of SI may have been with the military, the essence of SI applies to all organizations — that is, how organizations can improve their strategic decision-making process.

The answer to this question is being partly addressed by this book. Specifically, the convergence and application of knowledge management (KM), business intelligence (BI), and competitive intelligence (CI) can lead to the development and implementation of SI. In a 2001 survey of 500 senior executives, conducted by Knowledge Systems and Research Inc., asking about their SI needs, Ben Gilad in his *Early Warnings* book (American Management Association/AMACON, 2004) states some of the findings:

- 87 percent said their major intelligence-related problem was rapidly gathering intelligence to support critical decisions
- 68 percent reported the key intelligence-related issue for executives was obtaining 24/7 CI alerts distributed to appropriate endpoint users

These few statistics exemplify the role for CI and early warning systems to help executives plan for the future as part of their strategic decision-making process.

Ben Gilad (*Early Warnings*, AMACON, 2004) further discusses the concept of *strategic risk*, which he defines as the risk that the strategy itself is misaligned with market conditions. Gilad suggests that executives typically deal with financial, operational, and asset-impairment risks well, but they have a hard time handling the "competitive" strategic risk. Gilad indicates that industry dissonance is the most neglected risk and this is where top executives are most vulnerable. Human insight is needed to address industry dissonance, not just simply using technology.

To help reduce this risk, executives can use structured decision-making approaches such as multicriteria decision making. Executives are typically faced with multicriteria decision making when addressing strategic decisions. The alternatives used in multicriteria decision making are often competing, and there are numerous criteria to be factored into the decision-making process. To provide some SI to senior leader decision making, human insight and gut feeling can be augmented by applying techniques to help structure one's decision-making process. We have already highlighted the use of SWOT analysis, the balanced scorecard, scenario planning, etc., to help senior leaders better structure their decision process for making informed decisions.

One multicriteria decision-making-based approach that can be very useful to help quantify subjective judgments in decision making is the Analytic Hierarchy Process (AHP), which was developed by Thomas Saaty (University of Pittsburgh). The goal of the decision is first determined, and then criteria and subcriteria are developed, as well as various alternative solutions. A tree hierarchy is created with the goal at the top, the criteria and subcriteria in the middle, and the alternatives at the lower level. Through pairwise comparisons, the criteria are compared and weighted against each other with respect to the goal. This creates weights on the criteria that sum to one. Then, the alternatives are compared with respect to each criterion to get the weighting of the alternatives per criterion. Finally, a synthesis is made where the weights of the criteria and the weights of the alternatives per criterion are combined to get an overall weighting and ranking of the alternatives. This approach has been used by hundreds of organizations throughout the world to help them better structure their decision-making process, especially for strategic type of decisions.

To show how this approach may be applied, Liebowitz used the AHP recently to help an organization decide which document management system/portal tool would be the best choice to meet its strategic KM goals. Seven tools were considered: Autonomy, EMC Documentum, Hummingbird,

Plumtree, SharePoint, Interwoven, and LiveLink. The organization was interested in providing a way to reach out internationally to its customers for better sharing of information and knowledge. Expert Choice (www.expertchoice.com) is a tool that automates the AHP and was used to help the decision makers think through the process and tradeoff analysis. Essentially, all these leading tools could have done the job, but given some of the budgetary and technical constraints imposed by the not-for-profit organization, we were able to come to a ranking of the alternatives as shown in Figure 6.1. The criteria shown are: cost of the product, document management capabilities, collaboration capabilities, scalability, integration/migration, vendor support, and ease of use. Share-Point had the highest overall ranking after the synthesis and was thus considered the best choice.

SI: Where It Helps

A famous line from the musical *Pippin* is, "it's smarter to be lucky than it's lucky to be smart." Of course, it helps to have both intelligence and luck, but some decision makers go on their instincts to make the best choice. Part of these "instincts" is grounded in experience (perhaps called lessons learned/KM), CI, and BI. As we have been discussing throughout the book, these three areas form the basis for SI.

Where can SI help the decision maker? First, by applying KM, CI, and BI concepts, the strategic risk, as discussed by Ben Gilad, should be greatly reduced. CI will help better assess the competition and market conditions. KM can help leverage knowledge internally and externally, reaching out to customers and stakeholders. BI can provide an internal focus to apply data-warehousing and data-mining techniques to uncover hidden patterns and relationships in large masses of data. The KM, CI, and BI approaches provide the one-two-three punch by allowing the decision maker to get insights into the internal and external business environments.

A second area where SI can aid the decision maker is the ability to make better informed decisions with greater speed and confidence. In Shaku Atre's article, "The Top 10 Critical Challenges for Business Intelligence Success" (*Computerworld*, White Paper, June 30, 2003), she indicates that more than half of all BI projects fail owing to (p. 3):

- Failure to recognize BI projects as cross-organizational business initiatives
- Unengaged business sponsors who have little or no authority in the organization
- Unavailable or unwilling business representatives

To determine which Document Management System/Portal to buy
Details for Synthesis of Leaf Nodes with respect to GOAL

LEVEL 1	LEVEL 2	LEVEL 3	LEVEL 4	LEVEL 5
-------	-------	-------	-------	-------

COST   =0.265
.   AUTONOMY =0.017
.   SHAREPT =0.136
.   PLUMTREE =0.018
.   INTERWOV =0.021
.   HUMMINGB =0.033
.   DOCUMENT =0.013
.   LIVELINK =0.027
DOC MGT =0.252
.   AUTONOMY =0.066
.   SHAREPT =0.014
.   PLUMTREE =0.014
.   INTERWOV =0.021
.   HUMMINGB =0.052
.   DOCUMENT =0.052
.   LIVELINK =0.034
COLLABOR =0.172
.   AUTONOMY =0.009
.   SHAREPT =0.041
.   PLUMTREE =0.056
.   INTERWOV =0.009
.   HUMMINGB =0.019
.   DOCUMENT =0.010
.   LIVELINK =0.028
SCALABTY =0.073
.   AUTONOMY =0.013
.   SHAREPT =0.008
.   PLUMTREE =0.012
.   INTERWOV =0.007
.   HUMMINGB =0.011
.   DOCUMENT =0.010
.   LIVELINK =0.011
INT/MIGR =0.088
.   AUTONOMY =0.014
.   SHAREPT =0.005
.   PLUMTREE =0.014
.   INTERWOV =0.014
.   HUMMINGB =0.014
.   DOCUMENT =0.014

Figure 6.1   Synthesis of the results using Analytic Hierarchy Process/Expert Choice.

```
.        LIVELINK =0.014
VEND SPT =0.056
.            AUTONOMY =0.007
.            SHAREPT  =0.018
.            PLUMTREE =0.006
.            INTERWOV =0.007
.            HUMMINGB =0.007
.            DOCUMENT =0.004
.            LIVELINK =0.007
EASE USE =0.094
.            AUTONOMY =0.023
.            SHAREPT  =0.014
.            PLUMTREE =0.014
.            INTERWOV =0.005
.            HUMMINGB =0.019
.            DOCUMENT =0.005
.            LIVELINK =0.014
```

Synthesis of Leaf Nodes with respect to GOAL

OVERALL INCONSISTENCY INDEX = 0.05 (should be .10 or lower)

AUTONOMY 0.149 _____

SHAREPT 0.236

_____

PLUMTREE 0.134 _____

INTERWOV 0.085 _____

HUMMINGB 0.155 _____

DOCUMENT 0.107 _____

LIVELINK 0.134 _____

1.000

Figure 6.1 (continued)   Synthesis of the results using Analytic Hierarchy Process/Expert Choice.

- Lack of skilled and available staff or suboptimal staff utilization
- No software release concept (no iterative development method)
- No work breakdown structure (no methodology)
- No business analysis or standardization activities
- No appreciation of the impact of dirty data on business profitability
- No understanding of the necessity for and the use of metadata
- Too much reliance on disparate methods and tools

If these challenges are considered up front, then the likelihood of failure will greatly diminish. As these potential barriers are addressed at the beginning of the decision-making process, an informed decision will result from the BI, KM, and CI efforts.

KM also contributes to SI, and this synergy can allow lessons learned and best practices to help shape an executive's decision. Liebowitz developed an outline for a KM strategy and implementation plan to be aligned with an organization's (we will use XXX CORP as the pseudonym) strategic goals, as shown in Table 6.1. The KM strategy addresses people, process, and technology.

The KM strategy and implementation plan, with associated outcome measures, can provide the necessary knowledge to enhance the organization's strategic goals. KM is a key determinant of SI and ultimately can help organizations provide better, quicker decisions.

An Analogy for SI

Most people can relate to sports. Let us look at how SI can help a professional football team owner's strategic decision-making process. The strategic goals of the owner of a professional football team are probably to win the Super Bowl, make money, and have the team be recognized as a leader in the community. The synergy between KM, BI, and CI can provide the impetus for the generation of SI. CI, for example, might look at the players that could be drafted, traded, or picked up as free agents and how other teams might be vying for these players. Knowing what other teams might want may help your team become stronger by working out deals or trades and seeing how you can fill the gaps you need in your lineups. BI can provide all the statistical analysis needed to determine who to select in the draft or even to provide data-mining capabilities to help scout out players and determine the best fit within your organization (actually, a program called Scout already does this for the National Basketball Association). KM can provide leverage by learning through previous lessons (e.g., poor trades, good ones, right moves for team chemistry, coaching lessons, etc.) and to provide a strong sense of belonging

Table 6.1   Using KM to Contribute to SI

KM Strategy and Implementation Plan for XXX Corp
1. KM Supports Two Key XXX Corp Strategic Goals (Paraphrased)
Build community through collaboration
Create and share knowledge to stimulate innovation and promote community and business development
2. KM Components
People: Building and nurturing a knowledge-sharing culture
Process: Systematically capturing and sharing critical knowledge
Technology: Creating a unified knowledge network
3. People: Organizational Component
Chief knowledge officer (CKO) (or chief learning officer)
XXX Corp KM Council (chaired by CKO)
Full-time knowledge stewards in each department
Reassign roles/people at XXX Corp to be part of the KM initiative
A. CKO
Reports to executive director
Chairs the KM council
Spearheads KM strategy and KM initiatives for XXX Corp internally and externally
Strives to develop XXX Corp into a learning organization through people, process, and technology
B. KM Council
Comprised of the knowledge stewards in each department, region representatives, representatives from communications, HR, IT, strategy, policy, grants management, and library (new) (chaired by the CKO)
Meets each month to provide input and advice to the CKO regarding KM directions, project status, and success measures
C. Roles of the Knowledge Stewards
Responsible for leading and coordinating the KM activities within their respective departments

Table 6.1   Using KM to Contribute to SI (continued)

KM Strategy and Implementation Plan for XXX Corp
Conduct knowledge capture sessions, on a quarterly basis, involving experts within his or her department whose knowledge is "at risk" of being lost (e.g., institutional knowledge) and those in the department who have announced their retirement (incorporate this knowledge into the document management system)
Responsible for encouraging personnel in his or her department to enter and update their entries in the (to be developed) expertise locator directory at XXX Corp
Enlist, coordinate, and input the writing of best practices/lessons learned in their department and externally to be included in the best practices/lessons-learned repository (document management system and virtual best practices center)
Extract the respective department news on a weekly basis to be included in the intranet
Populates content in the intranet and XXX Corp Web site
Perform "after-action reviews" on projects to elicit and capture key learnings for posting in the lessons-learned repository
Analyze and interpret grant summaries to send to communications for dissemination/posting
Serve on the KM Council
D. Other KM Roles at XXX Corp
New library (with library specialist): works with intranet/Web colleagues in developing taxonomies; works with Communications in "pushing" relevant articles of interest to XXX Corp staff; assists XXX Corp staff in their research; serves as a repository of historical documents (also posted on intranet)
Communications: facilitates the dissemination of internal and external knowledge-sharing efforts
IT (needs to greatly enlarge the staff): handles the development and maintenance of intranet, document management system, expertise locator directory, best practice/lessons-learned system (virtual best practices center), and XXX Corp Web site
Human Resources: promotes learning and knowledge-sharing proficiencies as part of the recognition and reward system and the annual performance development plan; assists knowledge stewards, if necessary, in exit interviews; manages the mentoring program; coordinates, along with the CKO, the development and offering of XXX-Corp-wide minicourses in selected critical knowledge areas ("hot topics," KM education, etc.), etc.

Table 6.1   Using KM to Contribute to SI (continued)

KM Strategy and Implementation Plan for XXX Corp
All departments: assign respected individuals to act as facilitators of online communities of practice; assign knowledge stewards; continue with informal knowledge-sharing sessions (e.g., learn and lunch), etc.
4. Process
Develop learning and knowledge-sharing competencies as part of the annual performance plans
Conduct more "open" meetings throughout XXX Corp
Have monthly learn-and-lunch knowledge-sharing sessions based on conference trip reports, hot topics, short tutorials, etc.
Encourage the continuation of cross-teaming and development of online communities
Start to embed KM processes as part of daily work activities (capturing and using lessons learned/best practices during the project life cycle, having relevant "storytelling" for the first 5 to 10 min of staff meetings, having after-action reviews at the end of each project, etc.)
Develop a process and system to capture, analyze, interpret, and mine grant outcomes to inform strategy (two-year effort)
Establish a knowledge-sharing and recognition day (with associated awards) with XXX Corp and external community
Develop knowledge fairs/knowledge exchanges with the external community on selected topics of interest
5. Technology
Develop the taxonomy for the intranet, document management system/portal, and XXX Corp Web site
Develop the intranet (be sure to include a calendar of internal meetings/conferences/events, cheat sheets, online training modules, Excel/Word forms developed internally, PowerPoint slides, access to knowledge resources, meeting minutes/summaries, reports, synopses of XXX Corp reports, etc.)
Create an expertise locator system to be included as part of the intranet (internal and external contacts) — six-month effort
Develop a best practice/lessons-learned system for internal and external usage (see http://llis.nasa.gov as an example) — one-year effort
Develop a process and system to capture, analyze, interpret, and mine grant outcomes to inform strategy (two-year effort)

Table 6.1   Using KM to Contribute to SI (continued)

KM Strategy and Implementation Plan for XXX Corp
Start online communities
6. Three-Year KM Implementation Plan
Year 1
Appoint CKO, KM Council, knowledge stewards, and library specialist (establish XXX Corp library)
Reassign roles of existing staff in all departments (as given earlier) to support KM activities (Communications group plays an active central role)
Develop learning and knowledge-sharing competencies as part of the annual performance plans
Develop the taxonomy for the intranet and document management system/portal
Build the first version of the document management system (six-month effort)
Develop the intranet (be sure to include a calendar of internal meetings/conferences/events, cheat sheets, online training modules, Excel/Word forms developed internally, PowerPoint slides, access to knowledge resources, meeting minutes/summaries, reports, synopses of XXX Corp reports)
Create an expertise locator system to be included as part of the intranet (internal and external contacts) — six-month effort
Have monthly learn-and-lunch knowledge-sharing sessions based on conference trip reports, hot topics, short tutorials, etc.
Conduct more "open" meetings throughout XXX Corp
Establish a formal mentoring program
Encourage the continuation of cross-teaming and development of online communities
Start to embed KM processes as part of daily work activities (capturing and using lessons learned/best practices during the project life cycle, having relevant "storytelling" for the first 5 to 10 min of staff meetings, having after-action reviews at the end of each project, etc.)
Year 2
Develop a best practice/lessons-learned system for internal and external usage (virtual best practices center) (see http://llis.nasa.gov as an example) — one-year effort

Table 6.1   Using KM to Contribute to SI (continued)

KM Strategy and Implementation Plan for XXX Corp
Continue development of the document management system/portal (further populate content, increase online communities)
Develop a process and system to capture, analyze, interpret, and mine grant outcomes to inform strategy (two-year effort)
Establish a knowledge-sharing and recognition day (with associated awards) with XXX Corp and external community
Evaluate, continue, and expand year-1 KM efforts
Year 3
Evaluate year-2 KM efforts
Continue developing the system for analyzing, interpreting, and mining grant outcomes to inform XXX Corp strategy
Expand the number of online communities
Develop knowledge fairs/knowledge exchanges with the external community on selected topics of interest
Continue with relevant year-1 and year-2 KM efforts
7. Sample Outcome Measures for KM Initiatives
Savings or improvement in organizational quality and efficiency
Captured organizational memory
Reduced time to find relevant information and people
Increased sense of belonging and community among employees in the organization
Adapt quickly to unanticipated changes
Improve communication and coordination across XXX Corp
Improve innovation and business development per the XXX Corp loans given
Increase "customer" satisfaction

between the owner, coaches, players, and staff. All three elements — CI, BI, and KM — allow the owner to apply the SI to make his or her team a winner. Of course, besides personnel roles, there are many other elements that need to be considered to meet the owner's strategic goals, such as advertising or television right deals, negotiations with players and staff, facility/stadium improvements or selling rights, pricing arrangements for ticket holders, vendor deals, franchising arrangements, community support programs, etc.

Social Network Analysis: An Important Technique for Building SI

According to Rob Cross' (2004) book, *The Hidden Power of Social Networks,* networks of informal relationships have a critical influence on work and innovation. Research shows that appropriate connectivity in well-managed networks within organizations can have a major impact on performance, learning, and innovation. One way to better understand these informal relationships is through a technique called *social network analysis* (SNA) [Liebowitz, 2005]. SNA allows for a mapping of knowledge flows in organizations to identify key knowledge sources, sinks, and relationships (links/ties) between the actors/nodes (individuals/units) in an organization.

SNA usually follows six key steps [Cross, 2004]:

1. Identify a strategically important group.
2. Assess meaningful and actionable relationships (e.g., relationships that reveal collaboration in a network, information-sharing potential of a network, rigidity in a network, well being and supportiveness in a network, etc.).
3. Visually analyze the results (typically done through SNA software such as NetMiner, Inflow, UCINet-Netdraw, Pajek, etc.).
4. Quantitatively analyze the results.
5. Create meaningful feedback sessions.
6. Assess progress and effectiveness (usually a follow-up post-audit is conducted six to nine months after the network analysis is first conducted).

In step 4, there are individual network and group measures that are frequently used in analyzing the results. Individual network measures include various types of centrality. For example, *in-degree* centrality refers to the number of incoming ties a person has for a given relationship. Someone with a high in-degree centrality is a most sought after individual. *Out-degree* centrality is the number of outgoing ties a person has for a given relationship. Someone with a high out-degree centrality seeks advice or guidance from others and typically tries to communicate and collaborate with others. *Betweenness centrality* is the extent to which a particular person lies between the various other people in the network — those individuals with high betweenness centrality values could affect knowledge flows in networks if they were to leave. *Closeness centrality* is the extent to which a person lies at short distances to many other people in the network. Individuals highly central with respect to closeness tend to hear information sooner than others [Cross, 2004].

Group measures such as density and cohesion are often used in SNA. *Density* is the number of individuals who have a given type of tie with each other, expressed as a percentage of the maximum possible. If each person were connected to every other person in the network, the density would be 100 percent, or 1.0. *Cohesion* is the average of the shortest paths between every pair of people in the network. The average cohesion score should be about 2 in groups in which managers are interested in employees leveraging each other's expertise [Cross, 2004].

Geodesic distances between pairs of actors are the most commonly used measure of closeness. Geodesic distance is the minimum distance between actors. For example, I could send e-mail directly to Jim (path of length 1) or I could send my message for Jim to Kathryn (because Kathryn has Jim's e-mail address) and ask Kathryn to forward it to Jim (path of length 2). I would choose to send directly to Jim because the geodesic path would be lower and would often be the "optimal" connection between two actors. Usually, multidimensional scaling or component factor analysis are used to lay out the nodes.

There are different types of networks in organizations. Three of the major network types are the star, line, and circle. Generally speaking, actors with more ties have more "power" and greater opportunities because they have choices. In other words, there are alternate ways to satisfy needs and be less dependent on other individuals. There are also cliques and cutpoints. A *clique* is a subset of actors who are more closely tied to each other than they are to actors who are not part of the group. *Cutpoints* refer to the structure or network that would become divided into unconnected systems or networks if a node was removed.

Through SNA, different types of individuals could be identified in the network. *Central connectors* refer to the ones with the most arrows pointing toward them. These individuals could be the power players, unsung heroes, or the bottlenecks, depending on the situation. Boundary spanners provide critical links between two groups of people that are defined by functional affiliation, physical location, or hierarchical level. *Information brokers* are indirect connections, and they play brokering roles that can hold together entire groups. *Peripheral specialists* have one connection each and are not linked to each other (sometimes called *isolates*). Some people are "stuck" (e.g., newcomers) on the periphery and others may "choose" (e.g., experts) to be on the periphery [Cross, 2004].

By applying SNA, social groups and positions in groups can be visualized by considering the strength of connections between individuals (proximity data). SNA and knowledge-sharing/KM techniques (e.g., online communities of practice, lessons-learned/best practice systems, expertise locators, and others) can enhance the organizational learning environment. SNA can contribute to building SI because the real power in the organization can be mapped through the informal social networks to look at the centrality of power in the organization.

An Example Using SNA

SNA, via the mapping software Netdraw and UCINET 6 [Borgatti et. al., 2002], was used to develop knowledge maps as part of a knowledge audit for an organization. For example, the three social networks on the following pages, Figures 6.2, 6.3, and 6.4, show the survey responses of the top two individuals in an organization that people go to when they have questions or seek general advice. From these social networks, it is easy to view key individuals (such as Kevin S., Beard, Fossi, and others) whose knowledge is sought with respect to providing general advice. The sizes of the nodes are proportional to their betweenness centrality. That is, the larger the nodes, the more power the individual has because more people depend on that individual to make connections with other people. Figure 6.4 depicts the multidimensional scaling method, which shows the clusters of connections. Here, the darker nodes depict the *cutpoints*, whereby if a node is removed, that structure becomes unconnected. The larger nodes are shown in the middle (with the smaller nodes on the periphery) to indicate the strength of the connections.

Figure 6.4 can also portray groupings to indicate the level of connectedness and interactions between divisions. For example, the grouping with Trent (node 16) indicates that all those individuals are within one particular division and that they seek help within this community. Other divisions seem to seek help from within their own communities/divisions. The graph also shows some gatekeepers who bridge different communities (such as Sheila M. [node 28] who is connected to two communities). One area for improvement is to have better interlinking among the divisions by having more interaction between the executive office and the various divisions, and also having communications play a greater interconnected role by linking with the various divisions. The communications division should probably have a more central role instead of being on the periphery, as depicted in the third graph. Cross-teaming will help in sharing knowledge across divisions.

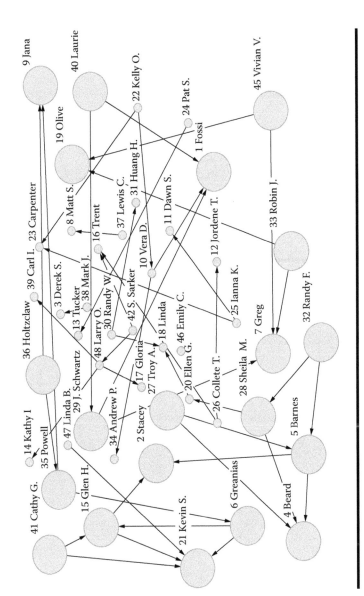

Figure 6.2 Connectedness and interactions between individuals.

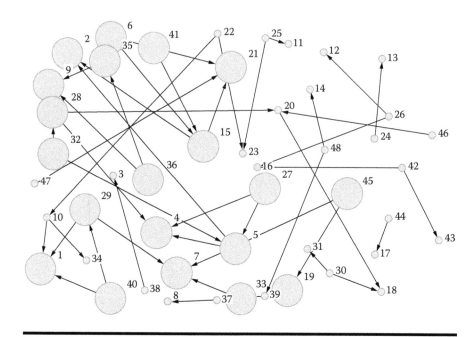

Figure 6.3 Another view of individual interactions.

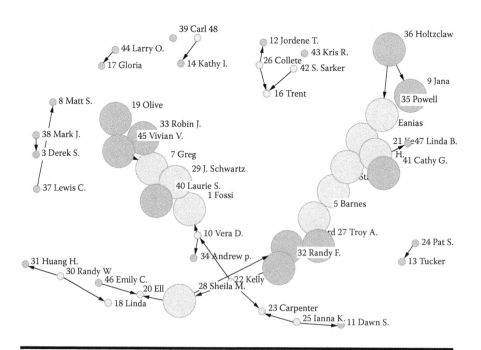

Figure 6.4 Multidimensional scaling of individual/division interactions.

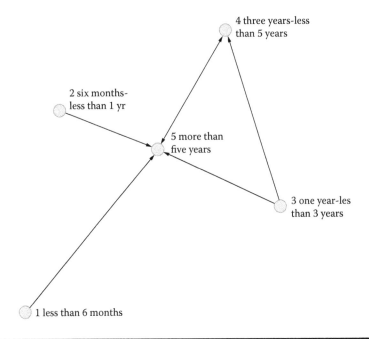

Figure 6.5   Interactions based on employee tenure.

SNA can also be used to see how the employees are interacting with each other based on their length of service to the organization. Figure 6.5 depicts the five communities of employees (those who have been at the organization less than six months, those six months to less than one year, those one year to less than three years, those three years to less than five years, and those more than five years). The social network shows a healthy relationship in that the newest employees in the organization seek advice from those who are typically fairly senior (more than five years at the organization). The organization may want to consider a mentoring program or buddy system whereby those employees who have been working less than one year can link up with those employees working one to three years (currently, those working less than one year in the organization are generally not seeking advice from their peers closest to their work experience) to further build a sense of belonging in the organization.

Summary

SI will be the catalyst for improved decision making of senior leaders. Through the synergy of KM, CI, and BI, SI will emerge and be one of the key determinants for successful decision making.

In the next section (Part II) of the book, cases will be discussed that apply KM, CI, or BI in their organizations to maximize the generation and level of their SI.

References

Borgatti, S.P., Everett, M.G., and Freeman, L.C., *UCINET 6.0*, Natick, MA: Analytic Technologies, 2002.

Cross, R., *The Hidden Power of Social Networks*, Harvard Business School Publishing, Cambridge, MA, 2004.

Liebowitz, J., Linking social network analysis with the analytic hierarchy process for knowledge mapping in organizations, *Journal of Knowledge Management*, Vol. 9, No. 1, 2005.

CASE STUDIES

II

Knowledge Management and Organizational Learning at the Annie E. Casey Foundation: A Case Study

Thomas E. Kern

Some Background on the Annie E. Casey Foundation: Helping Disadvantaged Kids and Their Families

The Annie E. Casey Foundation has been working to promote the well-being of vulnerable children and families for more than 50 years. Established in 1948 by UPS co-founder Jim Casey and his siblings to honor their mother, the Foundation's first grants supported a camp for disadvantaged children near the Casey family home in Seattle. Later, Jim Casey steered the Foundation's efforts toward finding more stable placements for children being bounced from one foster family to another.

In the 1980s, the Foundation shifted its focus toward improving the effectiveness of public systems — from education to child welfare to juvenile justice — that too often undermine families' strengths and create dependency. Today, the Foundation supports a diverse range of activities with a mission to build better futures for millions of American children at risk of poor educational, economic, social, and health outcomes. Its work is divided into three main areas: reforming public systems, promoting accountability and innovation, and transforming tough neighborhoods into family-supporting communities.

Headquartered in Baltimore, with a direct services component providing foster care and family services throughout New England, the Foundation makes grants that help states, cities, and neighborhoods fashion more creative, cost-effective responses to the challenges facing children and families whose circumstances place them at risk of not succeeding financially.

Knowledge Management and Organizational Learning: Challenges and First Steps

The Foundation's longstanding commitment to help disadvantaged kids and their families benefited significantly from an increase in its assets in the mid-1990s, a portion of which was directed to support funding for a larger staff and support more encompassing investments to develop comprehensive, integrated social strategies in a number of urban centers and also set up a strategic consulting arm to help states and localities make their public-service systems work better for children, families, and communities. This growth, along with the increasing complexity of the Foundation's work, posed challenges to its ability to take full advantage of the wealth of information and knowledge that its efforts were generating. In response, the Foundation's senior leadership authorized a study (first, an internal one in 2001, and then as the magnitude of the challenge became better known, a 2002 study drawing on external consulting support) of current knowledge practices at the Foundation and how well they supported its mission to help disadvantaged kids and their families.

The study began by identifying the obstacles to knowledge sharing that were impeding staff from breaking out of their program silos. An analysis and detailed staff survey brought several issues to the fore. First, accessing the most current and relevant knowledge across all programs was hindered by the lack of a centralized system for finding information. Second, staff members' heavy workloads meant that they had limited time to spend publicizing new knowledge, especially when there was no structured way for doing this. Third, Casey's organizational culture made over-reliance on informal (and, therefore, potentially less comprehensive) networks for exchanging knowledge the norm. Exemplified by its growing community work (see accompanying box), all of this was happening in an environment in which there were increasing demands of staff to have wider knowledge about related programs in addition to their own specialist skills. This was coupled with the understanding that if Casey was not sharing its expertise adequately with its own staff, it was likely not doing much better to leverage these resources with grantees, stakeholders, policymakers, and other Foundations.

The following is an excerpt from "Knowledge Management Comes to Philanthropy" by Marla M. Capozzi, Stephanie M. Lowell, and Les Silverman, *McKinsey Quarterly*, 2003 Special Edition:

> In 1999, the Casey Foundation concentrated some of its grants to launch *Making Connections,* an initiative to develop comprehensive and integrated social strategies in a few impoverished urban centers. The transformation meant that Casey had to hire new staff to support the expanded work. In addition, the role of its program officers, known as *senior associates,* changed: from being national, single-issue experts on subjects such as child welfare and juvenile justice, several became generalists leading cross-functional teams in one or two cities. Two problems, both relating to knowledge challenges, emerged as a result of these organizational moves. First, because the cross-functional approach meant that senior associates were now working in areas beyond their expertise, they needed more information from colleagues to do their work successfully. Moreover, many new staff members had a limited understanding of the history of the Foundation or the best practice it had learned over time. More often than not, they could get this information only by asking their longer-serving colleagues for it. What they needed to know wasn't written down; it had remained in people's heads. Second, what knowledge management there had been at the Foundation was in danger of diminishing. With the experts' time fragmented, no one took responsibility for managing the organization's knowledge in any single area. Meanwhile, senior associates, already busy in their cross-functional roles, were too distracted by requests for information from colleagues to begin generating and applying new knowledge to their grant-making and policy work.

Simply put, the 2002 study suggested that a large part of the valuable knowledge that Foundation initiatives were developing was not easily and readily obtainable and useable by staff, consultants, grantees, and colleague organizations, thereby undercutting its efforts to achieve its mission.

In some respects, the assessment amounted to a kind of business intelligence gathering for the Foundation. As a nonprofit organization, Foundations need this tool as much as businesses do to assess organizational performance against a set of measures that inform them of their effectiveness in achieving the outcomes they seek. The study also included a competitive intelligence component in which the practices of comparable organizations were benchmarked, affirming that most Foundations face the same challenges and identifying some model practices for the Casey Foundation to consider for its own use.

A Statement of Purpose, Core Elements, and Initial Priorities

The Casey Foundation's leadership believed that critical to its ability to address the needs of disadvantaged kids and their families and neighborhoods is its own understanding of (1) what works, (2) what it has learned in the past, and (3) how everyone can learn from each other, both within the Foundation and through partnerships with others. The 2002 study helped increase the Foundation's clarity around these challenges, and, with the study's findings and recommendations in hand, senior leadership created a new department, *knowledge services*, locating it within the Foundation's strategic consulting group to implement the study's recommendations. The Foundation hired a senior associate to assume overall responsibility and manage knowledge services' daily operations, which was built on the pre-existing library function now to be transformed to address a range of knowledge management (KM) and organizational learning activities. Knowledge services worked with several key departments such as information technology (IT), evaluation, and communications to operate within their framework and draw on their expertise to implement a KM strategy.

Supported by the study's findings and senior leadership input, the new knowledge services team identified the purpose of KM and organizational learning at Casey:

Improve access to Foundation knowledge, promote better understanding of the nuance and scope of the Foundation's learning journey and, where possible, facilitate the effective creation and leveraging of relevant knowledge.

In practical terms, the team proceeded from the understanding that KM is about the Foundation's capturing, organizing, and sharing the knowledge it needs for its work. It began with six key elements in mind to help guide its efforts. These had come out of the 2002 study:

1. Develop an organized knowledge architecture for staff to access knowledge across multiple program areas while creating new knowledge relevant and organized for users. Benefits would include the ability of staff to more easily and rapidly browse for the knowledge they need, greater consistency in the formats for knowledge creation, and clarity around how the Foundation might wish to direct its investments in knowledge development and cross-cutting activities.

2. Leverage technology to support KM to help improve knowledge creation and sharing by centralizing these activities for knowledge creators and improving their distribution for users. If accomplished, this could provide authors with one central location to input knowledge into their taxonomies, maintain a single place to look with knowledge requests, and offer centralized administration of the systems to ensure continuous upgrading based on user needs and available technology.

3. Establish robust KM processes to ensure systematic implementation across the Foundation. Key benefits to this work are the assurance that all knowledge areas are organized consistently, that gaps in knowledge, if they exist, can be more readily identified and acted upon, and that routine procedures will ensure that new resources are collected regularly to maintain currency.

4. Clarify KM roles in the Foundation to allow it to organize and implement KM successfully against specified goals. Benefits here are focus for the work and reduction of redundancy, a helpful delineation of expectations and responsibilities, and the dedication of full-time resources to a central function that ensures experts throughout the Foundation have effective support.

5. Foster a learning and teaching culture to ensure a strong organizational basis to support and encourage ongoing KM initiatives. Learning programs and curriculum can help facilitate knowledge sharing, supported by job descriptions and performance standards and evaluations that emphasize their value and importance.

6. Set strategic KM objectives supported by leadership to help ensure senior management focus and alignment with the Foundation's mission. If staff understands senior leadership's support for the work and its alignment with Foundation priorities, theirs will match it.

These elements would eventually infuse much of Casey's development of its knowledge tools and services.

The 2002 study recommended a number of specific actions, primary among them the creation of a flagship, Web-based KM system for Casey staff, consultants, and grantees. Equally important, although less resource and time intensive, was the call to integrate the Foundation's library services with KM, provide support to help staff in their knowledge development and documentation efforts, develop a range of tools to improve awareness and integration of Casey programs, and be attentive to the longer-term challenge of supporting the Foundation's efforts as a learning organization.

With a new department, a statement of purpose, a set of guiding core elements, and initial priorities in place, the Foundation officially began its KM implementation in early 2003.

Building a KM System: A Whole Greater than the Sum of Its Parts

Casey made its first priority the creation of an easy-to-use system that could be integrated into staff's daily work and accessible from one's desktop or from the road. The result was the KM system, which enabled each grant-making and direct services arm staff member to capture and organize resources pertinent to his or her work and, at the same time, have immediate, electronic access to search and download documents pertaining to that work as well as all of the Foundation's knowledge areas. The system was built on a Microsoft application called *SharePoint* (version 2), which was launched in late 2003.

The KM system was created by first customizing taxonomy maps for each knowledge area. Two dozen customized taxonomies were organized around best practice principles, system reform themes in public human service delivery, the Foundation's own program initiatives, and base knowledge in each knowledge area. These headings served as buckets to capture all the documents relevant to that knowledge area.

Next, the knowledge services team gathered knowledge resources that were already captured in a useable format from multiple sources. It did this by conducting an initial, retrospective information audit of resources in which documents made available by staff were profiled and added to the KM system. Over 6000 documents were entered into the KM system in the first year. A major challenge was for the system to reflect Casey's knowledge in an up-to-date way; therefore, users were asked to make ongoing contributions to the system as new resources became available.

The KM system was intended to address many of the issues raised by the 2002 survey of Casey staff. Whereas staff had indicated that they often worked in program silos isolated from the work of others, the KM system sought to improve the flow of resources across programs or knowledge areas by clearly and consistently organizing knowledge resources in each area and improving their accessibility to everyone. Improved information sharing was meant to inform Casey's work in a couple of ways. The KM system was not only designed to help quickly orient newcomers to Casey, it also served as a reference point for questions about Casey's point of view in any of the knowledge areas, or as a place to look for key readings on a subject of importance to Foundation staff. The KM system also offered an opportunity for all staff members to share experiences, lessons learned, and templates on how to capture and distill the work. The intent was that this would lead, where needed, to the identification of opportunities to explore new areas or fill gaps in the Foundation's or the field's thinking. Overall, by improving its ability to acquire and share knowledge and by leveraging its knowledge base, the Foundation would be able to more effectively and directly have impact, influence, and leverage in the areas that matter most so that it achieves better outcomes for disadvantaged kids, their families, and the neighborhoods in which they live.

The KM system was designed as a road map, in that it graphically arrayed each knowledge area with the taxonomy developed by the experts and the KS team. So, in response to the widespread request of Foundation staff, the KM system shared a snapshot, area by area, of what the Foundation is about. Although not meant to be a document management system, knowledge services designed the KM system to facilitate an expert's file management and ease of accessing items to forward in response to requests. Finally, the KM system was intended to serve as a vast electronic library that represented the Foundation's thinking in a dynamic and ongoing way. With the capability to easily enter new documents, the KM system offered a window on the cutting edge of the Foundation's work and research. At the same time, it provided access to documents from Casey's past, covering the scope of work and recording the progress and process of Casey's thoughts over the years.

Other useful tools in each knowledge area under the base knowledge category included:

- *Essential readings* that help users understand how Casey develops its point of view in the area.
- *News/events* in the area available through online connections to news services.
- *People/experts* as Foundation staff, TA providers, and experts in the field of the knowledge area. When possible, the expert's specialty and experience are listed.
- *Additional resources,* including other organizations, Web sites, and links relative to the knowledge area.

Illustrations of the main screens in the KM system follow, as shown in Figure 1.

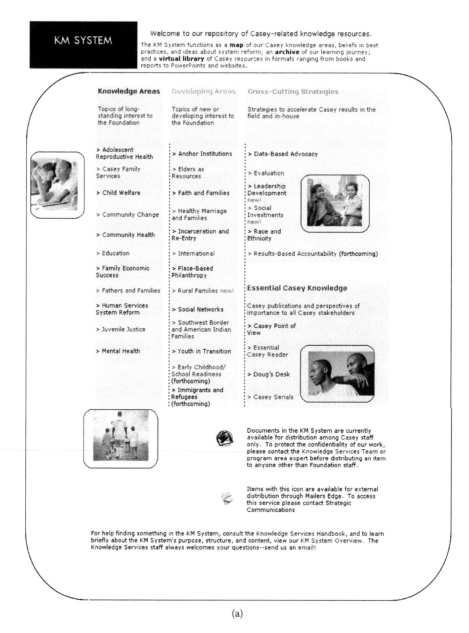

(a)

Figure 1 Illustrations of the main screens in the KM system.

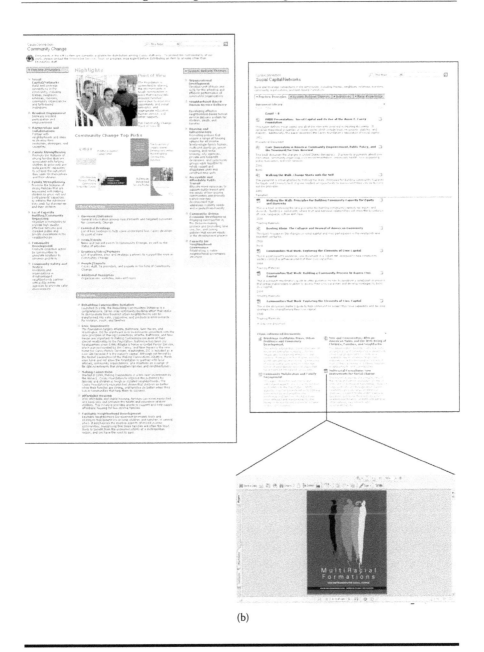

(b)

Figure 1   Illustrations of the main screens in the KM system (continued).

Integrating KM and the Library, Supporting Documentation, Increasing Awareness, and Furthering Organizational Learning

Knowledge services also addressed four other priorities in its first two years of work.

Integrating KM and the Library: Providing Unified Electronic Literature and Reference Services

The Foundation's longstanding library services were a natural for integration with its emerging KM work. Both functions were combined organizationally, and all tools and supports reorganized to make available to staff under the knowledge services mantle. Key library resources maintained, enhanced, or augmented under knowledge services included a range of desktop tools: general and specialized databases and online library catalogs, online newspaper access (including full text news, journals, news-clipping services, and Internet Web-site directories of content-rich Web sites relative to Casey's work). All these were accessible via the Foundation's intranet. Along with these online tools, knowledge services offered acquisition and reference services to staff.

Documentation Support

Many Foundation activities produce knowledge in the form of an exchange of ideas, data and information, and learnings that merit documentation or capture. Some knowledge comes from its own program experts or grantees, whereas other insights are derived from conversations between and the interactions of a combination of Casey staff, outside experts, practitioners, policymakers, and residents. Documentation can range from simple meeting capture to the significant evaluation work that is the Foundation's benchmark.

Effective documentation at all levels helps the Foundation better achieve the targets that it sets for itself. A good documentation product can help keep dialog open and running, record an emerging picture of work on the ground, codify our institutional memory, or offer insight to promising and best practices. In light of the Foundation's active documentation efforts across its programs and in the many products it develops, knowledge services developed its role in three ways. First, via the KM system for which it was responsible, it sought to create opportunities to include and share these products easily and efficiently with all staff. Second, it convened the Foundation's documentation workgroup — a monthly, organization-wide gathering of more than two dozen staff and close-in consultants who provided or frequently drew on documentation support. The group meets during the Foundation's "no-travel" week to share with each other the ongoing range of Casey documentation activities, to build on each other's experiences, and to consider new opportunities for some form of documentation in which needs might exist. The third role that knowledge services began to take on, informed by the rich conversation and sharing emanating from the documentation workgroup, was to help respond to previously unaddressed or new documentation needs throughout the Foundation. The collective experience of the documentation workgroup began to yield a range of documentation tools that could be formalized and made accessible to all staff. Knowledge services shared these documentation tools on the intranet, along with a documentation request form, that walked staff through the process of defining their documentation needs. Knowledge services took the view that the documentation process involved not only getting the right documenter for the job; it was also a matter of selecting the appropriate end product for the given audience and deciding on the appropriate degree of documentation for the given type of event. For this reason, the knowledge services intranet site explained the differences between documentation types, provided effective examples of each, and made format and template recommendations depending on the user's needs.

Tools to Improve Awareness and Integration of Casey Programs

Even the most advanced technology application requires the user to proactively go to the application to use it. E-mail alerts and desktop forcing mechanisms notwithstanding, the absence of a positive commitment to learn about and use these tools undercut their value.

Knowledge services designed several approaches in its first two years to increase awareness, interest, and an understanding of how to use its emerging KM tools. Individual and group training, written system documentation, promotional flyers and intranet stories, e-mail alerts, individualized reports to program experts and supporting staff — all can have some impact on increasing awareness and support for KM and organizational learning services.

One tool, in particular, that the Foundation took pride in was the creation of E-Casey, an internal monthly video newsletter accessible via its intranet (see Figure 2). E-Casey focused on timely issues of Foundation-wide interest and highlighted the interconnectedness of Casey's programs and initiatives. E-Casey's embedded links drew staff into the KM system and to useful Web sites and key documents through the Web links relevant to the video content embedded in the online screens. In addition to its

Figure 2   E-Casey.

role as an awareness and informational tool, E-Casey helped spur the Foundation's cataloging of video resources, particularly those that it had produced or funded itself. Further, knowledge services used E-Casey as an exit interview tool when staff left the Foundation to retire or move on to another position. This tacit knowledge capture complemented written or codified materials that may have already been in place.

The Casey Foundation as a Learning Organization

The KM system was designed to reduce staff reliance on informal networks as the sole or primary method by which staff exchanges information. However, by no means could or should it replace the kind of staff interaction and collaboration that is essential for focused conversations about Casey's work. These informed and focused conversations are necessary to support knowledge development and learning and implement the Foundation's work in the communities in which it is involved. That is why KM at Casey needed to be more than a KM system and what might be perceived as just a technology fix. The Foundation has learned from its colleagues in the field of philanthropy and from the emerging literature that KM can be a part of a larger organizational learning agenda that has value and daily application for everyone.

For Casey, organizational learning represented the enhanced intellectual and productive capability gained through institution-wide commitment to continuous improvement. It occurs through the exchange of insights and builds on the Foundation's ongoing assessment of what it and the field has learned and experienced. The Casey Foundation already benefited from several organized and thoughtful learning activities. From its Fellows Program and significant investments in evaluation to its use of cross-site learning exchanges, peer organization matches, consultative sessions, and staff development meetings, to the publication of ADVO-CASEY and *CaseyConnects*, Casey already developed or adapted a number of forums for effective learning, sharing, and collaborating. The effectiveness of these existing strategies begs the question of what else can the Foundation do? As the following model suggests, organizational learning can work with KM to improve awareness of existing Casey knowledge — whether it be in the form of documents or personal know-how (or tacit knowledge). To start, Casey has begun to look more intentionally across sectors to inform its work — for instance, bringing the Foundation's experience on neighborhoods and system reform in sync or sharing grantmaking and direct services experiences with each other. As the Foundation's KM practices have matured, senior leadership has called on knowledge services to identify additional ways in which staff can be given the time and space to apply learning principles in their work. This will become a significant part of knowledge services' workload over the next two years.

Early Evaluative Measures: Evaluation in the Context of Results; What Have We Done, How Well Did We Do It, Is Anyone Better Off?

Evaluation in the Context of Results

By improving its ability to acquire and share knowledge and by leveraging its knowledge base, the Foundation will be able to more effectively and directly have impact, influence, and leverage in the areas that matter most so that it can achieve better outcomes for disadvantaged kids, their families, and the neighborhoods in which they live. The following scenario, taken from the 2002 study, identifies the kind of role that the KM system can play to help Casey improve how it does its work.

The Foundation's evaluation of its KM work during its first two plus years of operation have included several approaches. First, knowledge services has looked at usage of the KM system and other online tools, where tracking tools exist to measure it. Second, it has undertaken several surveys of staff and held consultative sessions that are able to yield

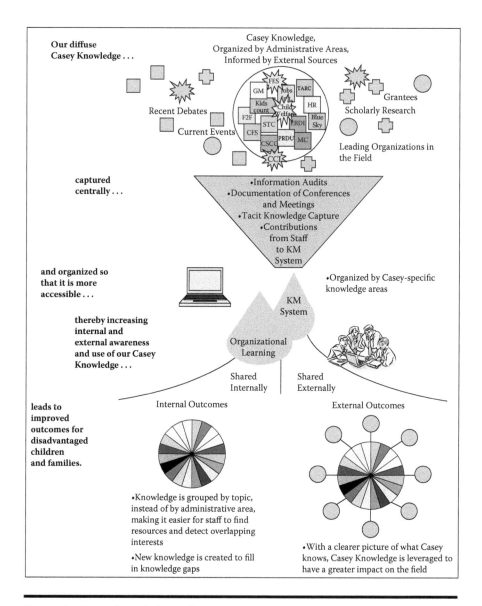

Figure 3   Casey knowledge culture.

qualitative data on staff satisfaction and suggestions for KM. These are baselined against earlier surveys to track progress. Third, it occasionally draws on consulting support to obtain internal and external perspectives on the Foundation's services and supports. As its knowledge services evolve, evaluation protocols will begin to assess progress in three areas: knowledge capture and organization, sharing, and application (see Figure 2). Examples of measures include (see Figure 4):

An example scenario

Before the KM system...	With KM initiatives...	Outcomes and results of KM...
"A staff member needs information about best practices and different approaches to building community schools in one of the MC sites." 1. Looks on the public Web site and after spending a remarkable amount of time, cannot find information/resources. 2. Raises questions at the following TARC help desk meeting (two weeks later) 3. Gets contacts/leads from other staff members 4. A peer match is suggested to meet the staff member's needs	**Process** • Consistent structure organizes knowledge/Casey expertise (e.g., Casey point-of-view and essential readings on program areas) • Procedures capture knowledge from the Foundation and the field • Templates for most important situations (e.g., lessons learned, how to's, learnings from peer materials) **Enablers** • Facilitators research requests and connect relevant knowledge to users **Technology** • KM system provide users with one entry point to search all knowledge in an easy and intuitive way	• Staff member searches the KM system and finds, in real time, best practices and strategies to build community schools • Finds codified knowledge from other MC sites (lessons learned and models pertinent to MC outcomes • Calls knowledge facilitator and gets additional contacts and Casey's latest thinking (work-in-progress) around community schools • Uses help desk for problem solving around outcomes and best approaches to get to the outcomes

• Staff are not fully leveraging Casey's expertise and often reach out to informal networks or outside expertise

• As a result, Casey misses the opportunity to inform policy with broad knowledge from the field

• People seeking information can rapidly identify and access Casey's point-of-view and existing knowledge within Casey and from the field

• Casey is able to leverage its knowledge from the field to better inform policy

Figure 4   Sample scenario of KM at Casey.

- ■ *Knowledge capture/organization* — The number of contributions to knowledge databases, the number of contributors, the breadth and depth of capture across all Foundation programs
- ■ *Knowledge sharing* — The formalization of professional development within the Foundation to mentor new staff and increase their institutional and program knowledge, number of formal and informal "communities of practice" taking place inside and outside the Foundation, the number of resources developed by Casey for external audiences, and the extent of their distribution
- ■ *Knowledge application* — The extent to which effective examples of the Foundation's work (best practices, lessons learned, case studies, etc.) are used, time and cost savings based on improvements to knowledge availability

An initial evaluation of the Foundation's KM initiative in the first full year of the KM system's operation and availability of the initial round of tools shows modest but increasing use of these services. Staff utilization has been shown to increase in tandem with continuing training of staff, ongoing promotional tools, and affirmation of these services by senior leadership. To build on this further, the Foundation's leadership has called on knowledge services to develop a strategy for incentives and recognition to use these services, encouraging everyone to take the time and space to build them into their daily regimen. Contributions to the KM system and to all the tools have been significant, far exceeding expectations. In fact, it affirms that Casey is a sharing culture, even though staff is still challenged about how best to draw on these resources to support the work.

Consensus exists to expand the scope of knowledge services (in particular, the KM system) to audiences outside the Foundation, including the general public as well as grantees, policymakers, and colleague organizations. Staff expect appropriate restrictions on resources to be shared, with attention given to the confidentiality and data sensitivity of certain materials. With wider access to those wanting to address the needs of disadvantaged kids and their families, the Foundation anticipates greater utilization and sharing of these resources.

Lessons Learned

Three years into the work, the Casey Foundation can point to several lessons learned, from which the work's further efforts can be directed.

The Work Is a Nonstarter without Senior Leadership Support

The Casey Foundation's KM initiative began and has continued with strong senior leadership support, including that of the president and managing fellow for Casey Strategic Consulting. Key program officers have also voiced and offered active support to the work. Senior leadership shared a vision of what difference the work could make, invested in it, stood behind it, and, accordingly, holds it accountable to this vision. Without these voices and the resources they have committed to, a new initiative such as this would be nothing more than an idea whose value remains underimplemented and untested.

Old Habits Die Hard

No matter how good or effective new tools and approaches to work might be, old habits die hard. New approaches remain an ideal, until each person can in his or her time and space embrace and fashion them to his or her own unique style and needs. Although it is cost-effective to design standardized systems to improve knowledge capture, organizing, and sharing, it is equally important to accommodate the nuances of as many individual staff as possible, helping them see how the tools can be applied to meet their unique perspective, working style, and idiosyncrasies. Going back to the previous subsection, staff must see that their leaders affirm and reward these new approaches, grounded in the overall vision of the organization, before they will change their behavior.

Technology Is Not the Answer, It Is the Question

Technology makes so much of the KM and organizational learning work possible where, in contrast to a few years ago, barriers such as the inability to cross reference items or link to different types of documents would have been nonstarters for systems attempting to cater to a range of user styles. However, technology is not the answer. It is a means to an end, not the end in and of itself. In fact, technology is the question. And the question is, given the outcomes we envision being most useful for us in support of our work and how it gets done, what should the technology be? When we work from existing applications and try to fit our own behavior to them, we make it even more difficult to attune our work habits to services that are meant to help us get things done. But if the applications can be fitted to our daily working needs and styles, nurtured with senior leadership expectations, training, and awareness-building services, the chances that these tools will catch on are strong.

Ready, Fire, Aim: Aka the Iterative, Prototyping Nature of the Work

Prototypers claim they build the plane as they fly it. Building a KM System for initial use before getting everything perfect is safer than flying in a partially built airplane, but is still risky, if in fact it misses or distorts the organizing principles a workplace needs to have addressed to improve its effectiveness. Nonetheless, lots of program or system design gets caught up in the need for perfection (the perfect is the enemy of the good, right?) in nuanced areas that simply reflect one person's or one style's preference (in this case, the decision maker rather than perhaps the users) over another. Sometimes it is best just to get some thoughtful but not overly designed tools out there for use and reaction as a better way to get feedback and continuous improvement, rather than extend the process through "ready, aim, aim, aim ...."

One Way or Another, KM Is a Cross-Functional Task, So Coordination Is OK and Necessary, and Accountability Shared

Organizations struggle with where to assign a function such as KM. In some places, it is part of IT. In others, it is tied to evaluation. In yet others, it is part of communications or human resources (HR). At the Casey Foundation, the work was integrated with the library function in a department unconnected to IT, HR, communications, or evaluation. In point of fact, KM would need to be coordinated with at least two or three services anyway, wherever it was located. The key is to get good at coordinating to begin with. As a centralized function, KM touches all aspects of the organization's life. Being able to interact with, accommodate, and be responsive to all parts of an organization is the critical success factor.

Keeping the End in Mind: Utilization and Answering the "So What?" Question

Although it can be painful to look at the utilization rate of knowledge services in the early stages of an initiative such as KM, it is a realistic and necessary part of the learning journey toward building tools and supports that are useful. Evaluation metrics for this work are still in the developmental stage. Some of the better ones are qualitative, and it is difficult to assign a number to them. But if the work is not grounded in achieving the organization's purpose, with each decision made keeping this in mind, then KM loses its connection with the people and outcomes it is meant to serve. If the organization is not committed to, or if knowledge services are not geared toward, greater sharing of resources, then these barriers will result in limited utilization of resources by internal and external users alike.

Next Steps

Much has been accomplished in the three years since Casey engaged an external consultant to both assess its KM and organizational learning practices and suggest a course of action. These accomplishments involved the creation of a number of tools and supports that staff, consultants, and eventually grantees and colleague organizations could draw on for improving their efforts to help disadvantaged kids and their families. Equally important, attentiveness to the learning conversation throughout Casey has underscored an already rich array of organizational learning approaches that the Foundation has developed over the years, independent of a formal KM/organizational learning initiative. The continuing development and refinement of knowledge tools and a critical mass of learning efforts against which Casey can baseline its organizational learning goals makes for a timely launching point to take the work even further, with the prospect that an organizational learning strategy or curriculum may help provide a framework in which the work can be focused even more purposefully than before.

The Foundation's initial work around an internally focused KM system will lead to new challenges. One is making the KM system available to the public. In 2005, communications, IT, and knowledge services are working closely to complete an overhaul of the Foundation's public Web site, with an integral "knowledge center" through which a variety of public audiences can access knowledge resources related to their interests.

Another challenge for the Foundation is to improve its tacit knowledge capture and sharing. Codified or written knowledge resources represent what the KM field calls the explicit side of knowledge that a KM system can capture, organize, and share. However, the notion of tacit knowledge (the know-how represented by the people who write about or do the work and knowing how to get hold of them) is equally important in its own way. The Foundation's leadership has called on knowledge services to build a talent bank or expertise system that gets at several ways of representing this know-how: the experts in fields that matter to Casey. This will be a component of the existing KM system, but require different ways of thinking about the information, collecting it, and keeping it current.

The larger challenge remains: creating and sustaining an organizational and community culture in which everyone participates to access and share knowledge resources seamlessly and routinely. Advances in technology make it easier than ever to support such a culture. Results accountability helps structure the work to highlight where effective information and knowledge resources can best be used in achieving the program's goals. A vital mission motivates us all to help improve people's lives. Changing how we do our work to leverage these supports remains the single-most important factor for us and, ironically, the most easily changeable feature of our work environment if we seek the lasting changes our mission calls for. A leadership development expert has said that "all of us are smarter than some of us." Until we live up to that premise, we will never realize our full potential.

Note: The views expressed in this case study are the author's and do not necessarily reflect those of the Annie E. Casey Foundation.

Case Study in Strategic Scenario Development

Maritza Morales

Case Study:
Motorola 2010 Scenario Development

Introduction: The Problem/Opportunity

This case study is about the use of scenarios to define the strategic focus of Motorola, a leader in telecommunications industry (see the section in this chapter titled "Appendix: Company Background/Profile" for company background). The key strategic question raised by the management team was: should Motorola continue to invest heavily in Asia in the expectation that increasing shares of its revenues will come from the Far East? Or does the long-term outlook favor the United States or Europe?

At the time, Southeast Asia was experiencing tremendous economic growth (as measured by the gross national product, GDP). In addition, globalization forces were shaping the political and economic evolution of all regions, especially Asia. This resulted in a general consensus among executives that Southeast Asia was likely the most promising source of future revenues for the company (see Figure 1).

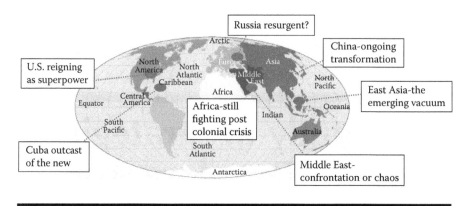

Figure 1   1993 geopolitical backdrop; the end of the bipolar world.

A thorough analysis of this underlying premise was deemed necessary to prioritize or align investments and other resources appropriately. It was important for the management team to separate myth from reality and identify the ways in which the circumstances could evolve around the world to diminish or create opportunities for Motorola.

Methodology

The only certain thing in the evolution of a thriving country or region is change. Thus, it was determined that attempting to forecast the developments of Motorola's regional markets would not provide a sensible direction for the future. Instead, the approach of *scenario planning,* created by the California-based Global Business Network (GBN), was chosen to enable the full understanding of possible external environments that would challenge Motorola's strategies and plans in the decades ahead.

Scenarios are powerful tools for developing the strategic vision of a business and to guide the strategy development process. By questioning assumptions about the way the world will act, decision makers are able to see the world more clearly. Scenarios are not for predicting the future, but rather for envisioning possible futures in the present. Scenario planning provides for a robust strategic framework to develop long-term strategy and make better decisions for the future. The principles of scenario planning are used by decision makers to:

■ Articulate and discuss the range of uncertainties that could affect the outcomes of their company's plans and strategies
■ Define the boundaries of these uncertainties in a way that will be most useful in making decisions

Motorola 2010 Scenario Process

The main objective of the Motorola 2010 scenario planning exercise was to recognize and prepare for changes, threats, and opportunities by identifying the most relevant and plausible scenarios that captured the evolution of the world's geopolitical climate, competitive/regulatory changes, and market dynamics.

The development of the 2010 scenarios encompassed a series of activities and the participation of many key individuals from the organization:

- Appointment of team members that could represent the perspectives of all businesses, all geographies, and all functions (such as human resources, finance, marketing, manufacturing, etc.)
- Executive consensus of the focal issue or problem to be addressed by the team
- Training of team on the principles of scenario development and rules of engagement (leave preconceived notions at home, think from the outside in, and do not prejudge options, etc.)
- Thorough research and analysis of current state of the economies and countries to be discussed across the United States, Europe, Asia, and the Pacific
- Two team-working sessions (one to two days each), as well as follow-up strategic sessions

By the end of the first team session, four plausible future scenarios had been outlined and described (see analysis segment for more details) and early warning indicators and implications identified. As a follow-up in preparation for the strategic planning sessions, the scenario assumptions were tested for relevance and validity in collaboration with external experts and analyzed in depth through various tools such as economic modeling. Following the analysis, scenario narratives were developed by the experts at GBN. Narratives are key in this process because they provide, in a story form, all the details necessary to visualize and prepare for the world in which each scenario would come to fruition ("This is a world in which …").

Scenario narratives were shared with the team before the strategic planning session to test insight and create a mind shift toward the possible futures outlined. In addition, the team was asked to decide which of the scenarios seemed most plausible for the company and represented their "official future." Once there was certain agreement as to the official future, the decision makers proceeded to formulate strategic options and recommendations that would position the organization to succeed under any or all four futures. An important last step was to develop action plans with ownership by team members for the implementation of the most relevant recommendations, with emphasis on the action items that applied to any/all scenarios. (These are termed the "no-brainer" recommendations in the context of scenario planning.)

Analysis and Alternatives

To best address the focal issue, the team was given some parameters:

- Emphasis was to be placed on social and economic evolution of the various regions, not on specific telecommunications markets.
- Discussions were to cover a very long-term horizon — from 1993 to 2010.
- Team members were to apply out-the-box thinking such that they would be able to anticipate major world/regional inflection points (of the likes of privatization of telecommunications, the shift of Europe toward a vision of integration, the post-Mao Chinese reforms, and the fall of communism).

The scenario session began with an extensive brainstorm and discussion exercise to identify and prioritize the key external factors that would play a major role in the future development of world regions. The resulting list of factors included:

- Relations with other countries on one hand, trade wars on the other
- Relationships with customers/partners
- Ability to deal with technological discontinuities — death/birth of new businesses
- Ability to synergize across businesses and regions
- Ability to overcome company biases
- The size of the opportunities
- Environmental threats

The team proceeded to discuss how these factors interact/differ and create uncertainties for the business. The core relationships were stated as:

- Technology versus relationships
- Globalism versus regionalism
- Economic fragmentation versus integration

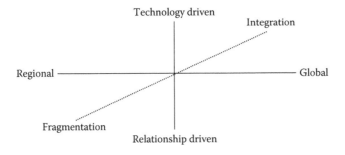

Figure 2   Scenario matrix.

The team agreed that these were the greatest uncertainties that could largely shape the characteristics of the world in which Motorola would operate in 2010. Once agreement was reached on these core factors, the interrelationships were plotted on a four-quadrant matrix (see Figure 2).

This resulting matrix was used as the framework to define four divergent scenarios that would help envisage and prepare for the company's future external environment, challenges, and opportunities. To define the scenarios (possible futures), the team began describing each of them according to the core matrix dimensions: whether the world focus was on technology or relationships, whether the world was fragmented or integrated, and whether the regions ruled over globalization. Key questions addressed during the initial definition of the four scenarios included: What trends would rule under each alternative? What would the world economy look like? What would be the relative economic strength of the various regions under each potential future? The results of this exercise are given in Figure 3.

Following agreement of the main driving forces of each scenario, the team proceeded to name the scenarios and describe in general terms what each of these alternative future world views would look like. For each plausible scenario depicted, business implications and early warning indicators were identified and discussed at length.

Scenario 1: Meritocracy

Major Characteristics

- Two major economic regions: a strong Asia Pacific community and a sluggish European Economic Community (EEC), which struggles to integrate East Europe, Russia, and North Africa into an expanded bloc.

Scenario 1:	Scenario 3:
- Technology driven	- Technology driven
- Regional integration	- Global integration
- Two-bloc world	- Borderless world
Pacific-Rim/Europe	- Restructured info-economy
Scenario 2:	Scenario 4:
- Relationship driven	- Relationship driven
- Regional fragmentation	- Global fragmentation
- Three-bloc world	- Economic hardship
NA/Pacific Rim/Europe	

Figure 3 Scenario driving forces.

Table 1 GDP Projections

	1990–1995	*1995–2000*	*2000–2005*	*2005–2010*
World	2.9	3.7	3.4	3.4
United States	1.8	2.6	2.4	2.5
Japan	3.1	3.2	3.0	3.0
EC	1.7	2.7	2.4	2.1
Asia	6.6	6.5	6.1	5.8
China	9.7	8.6	8.3	7.7

Source: Team economic modeling projections.

■ Strong trade among United States, China, Japan, and Southeast Asia generates greater wealth than the social capitalism model in an expanded Europe.

■ GDP projections (see Table 1)

Scenario Implications

- Least change from the existing direction
- Strategic alliances increase in importance
- Need for capital to achieve necessary scale increases
- Critical to make seed investments in highest-growth areas: China, Japan, Asia
- Even with dominance of Asia Pacific, should not ignore development of Europe

Early Warning Indicators

- Efficiency of international organizations, such as the International Monetary Fund (IMF), the General Agreement on Tariffs and Trade (GATT), others
- Move toward open standards
- Effectiveness of collective security
- Growth in inter-bloc trade
- Asia Pacific Economic Cooperation (APEC) body grows and prospers
- National Research and Education Networks (NREN) being built by private sector
- Deregulation of Baby Bells (United States) and PTT (ministries of communications of foreign countries)

Scenario 2: Managed Marriage

Major Characteristics

- Three major economic blocs: Asia, the EEC, and the North America Free Trade Agreement (NAFTA)
- Environmental problems, especially in South Asia
- Social capitalism grows strong and Europe prospers, spurred by lower intraregion trade barriers
- Japan, China, and South Asia suffer turmoil in many fronts: social conflict, environmental issues, AIDS, natural disasters, border disputes
- The United States expands trade to the North and South but limits trade with the East/West through carefully managed relationships
- Europeans create and manage institutions to address social and environmental problems
- GDP projections

	1990–1995	*1995–2000*	*2000–2005*	*2005–2010*
World	2.6	3.0	2.7	2.5
United States	1.7	2.4	2.1	1.9
Japan	2.9	2.3	1.7	1.9
EC	1.9	3.3	3.2	3.1
Asia	5.5	3.5	1.9	1.0
China	9.1	5.6	3.3	1.5

Source: Team economic modeling projections.

Scenario Implications

- Europe is the place to invest: need to capitalize on lower intra-Europe trade barriers
- Best market: North America, due to NAFTA
- Would require preparing to cut losses in Asia
- Competencies in lobbying, relationship building, and negotiation become essential

Early Warning Indicators

- Growth in intrabloc trade
- Russia stability
- Rise of anti-Western political parties in China
- Explosion of trade between Europe and Islamic countries
- Rapid growth of environmental resources management (ERM) initiatives
- Reinforcement of local content in media
- Breakdown of trade talks among the United States, Japan, and China
- Government control of NREN
- Newly industrialized countries (NIC) following Japan's pattern of maturing economy

Scenario 3: Market World

Major Characteristics

- Borderless world bound together by telecommunications

- Severe environmental problems leading to economic restrictions in 2000–2005
- Economic changes resulting in a green (environmentally conscious), information-intensive society by 2005–2010
- Lots of investment and growth in the information infrastructure
- GDP projections

Scenario Implications

- Increase importance in corporate statesmanship
- Change in emphasis from treaties to strategic alliances
- Lower cost of international communications
- Importance of strong positioning among high-growth areas: China, Asia

Early Warning Indicators

- Evolving environmental issues and crises
- Ecological losses
- Globalization of currency and securities markets
- Emergence of regional/universal currencies
- Growth in strategic alliances, fewer treaties
- Success of killer telecommunications services and devices: cellular, PDA, and wireless data

Scenario 4: Mordida

Major Characteristics

- Little economic growth, reduced investments
- None of the competing capitalisms can stop the disintegration of the social and political fabric
- Lots of social conflict, immigrants clash with residents
- Ethnic strife, famine, and corruption are everywhere
- Social survival takes precedence over environmental reforms and economic growth
- GDP projections (see Table 2)

Table 2 Mordida GDP Projections

	1990–1995	*1995–2000*	*2000–2005*	*2005–2010*
World	2.2	2.1	1.5	1.4
United States	1.7	2.1	1.7	1.4
Japan	2.3	1.4	1.3	1.9
EC	1.3	1.3	0.2	0.2
Asia	5.5	3.3	2.7	1.4
China	8.6	4.5	3.7	2.1

Source: Team economic modeling projections.

Scenario Implications

- You cannot plan for Mordida but you can act against it.
- These conditions would create further privatization; private sector would be held to higher standards.
- Scrutiny now leveled at top politicians will later fall on large corporations.
- Investments safer close to home in NAFTA markets.
- Virtue of provider becomes competitive advantage.
- Power moves from treaties to strategic alliances.

Early Warning Indicators

- Ineffective world response to social and political issues
- Increase use of Swiss bank accounts
- Many treaties, fewer strategic alliances
- Export of crime and terrorism
- Shift from income toward value added taxes
- Arms sales by regions

Conclusions

Once the set of alternative future scenarios were very well understood (per Table 3), the team pondered the following questions:

Table 3 Summary of Core Elements of Each Alternative Scenario

	Meritocracy	*Managed Marriage*	*Market World*	*Mordida*
Driving factor	Economic	Political	Economic	Black market/military
Economy	Strong Pac-Rim	Strong Europe	Best	Worst
Business/government relationship	Partnerships	Government guides business	Business leads government	Business eludes government
Trade	Moderately free	Protectionist	Free/open	Limited to informal routes
Business drivers	Scale, technology	Push strategies to protect home markets; relationships for access to new markets	Market pull	Flexibility and adaptability
Capitalism	Monolithic capitalism led by Asia; pulls United States into bloc	Social capitalism, strongest in Germany	*Laissez-faire* capitalism led by United States opens markets	Competitive capitalisms create market chaos

Source: Motorola Global Scenarios presentation, May 1993.

Which of These Scenarios Represented the "Official Future"?

Considering the robust growth rates in Asia at the time of the planning exercise (1993), the *meritocracy* scenario was deemed the scenario that best represented Motorola's "Official Future." However, this assessment was not absolute, and some believed that the relationship-driven world of *managed marriage* represented a very likely future for Motorola, and needed to be carefully considered.

An important consideration under the meritocracy scenario was that Japan's pursuit of a monolithic capitalism could lead to major mistakes, whereas continued population growth in Asia could cause sharp declines in per capita income, rising social tensions, and create overall instability for these economies. Thus, the possibility of the failure of monolithic capitalism (meritocracy) had to be considered, as well as the possible success of the European model of social capitalism (managed marriage). The idea of a unified Europe was not out of the question, especially considering how European diplomatic skills had helped restore a good degree of economic vitality to the region.

What Region Was to Become Most Important for Motorola?

According to results from economic modeling, the European region was to do well in three out of four scenarios, whereas Asia only would do well in two. However, it was agreed that this did not mean that the future of Europe was necessarily much brighter than the future of Asia. It was believed that this outcome needed to be validated by testing the assumptions underlying the future scenarios. Thus, the consensus was that although there was not enough reason to pull back from Europe, there were enough reasons to become more involved in Asia.

The importance of Asia was underscored by its vast pent-up demand for telecommunications infrastructure and basic services, by its geographic challenges (which favored wireless over landline telephony), as well as the region's explosive population and economic growth.

Strategic Response/Recommendations

A thorough review of the scenarios (official and alternate futures) and their implications was followed by a discussion of possible strategic responses: how the company should go about preparing for these future developments:

1. Pick one scenario and bet the company
2. Hedge across all scenarios

3. Become a learning organization
4. Modify existing strategy according to the lessons learned
5. Rank strategic options by risks and rewards
6. Look for vulnerabilities and bottlenecks
7. Reframe the industry
8. Pursue option of least regret
9. Identify predetermined elements

The answer was a combination of several of these options (2, 4, 5, 6, and 9). It was deemed important to identify the things that would not change (predetermined elements, such as ethical standards and customer relationship goals), whereas formulating strategic changes that would prepare the company for each and all of the possible outcomes. A clear understanding of the risks and rewards of options was also considered critical to best determine which strategies required adaptation. A well-thought-out strategy was to become the weapon to hedge the company against negative forces in any or all of the possible scenarios.

Recommendations That Applied to All Scenarios

■ Establish a three-prong strategy:

Leadership: Attain technical and standards leadership in key markets by delivering the highest quality in the industry (for infrastructure, devices, and services).
Brand development: Focus marketing efforts on developing the Motorola brand, especially in China and Asia.
Strategic alliances: Forge critical alliances with key operator customers and channel partners.

■ Support international bodies such as the WTO, IMF, and GATT, whose policies help create/sustain the open markets that Motorola needs to grow.
  – Get involved in promoting free trade and recommending types of communications that would maintain open markets.
  – Lead in standards initiatives aimed at reducing the cost of international communications.
■ Develop different investment strategies for different countries and regions.
  – Intensify investments in China and other areas of high growth in Southeast Asia.
  – Calibrate investments in Europe according to the stiffer market conditions: well-established competition, large installed base of communications infrastructure, and mature economies.

Recommendations That Applied to Select Scenarios

■ Adjust product strategy according to market conditions.
- Position to lead with infrastructure solutions where the opportunity exists (meritocracy, market world) and with devices/services where growth is limited (managed marriage, Mordida scenarios).
- Emphasize functionality over cost when creativity or technology breakthroughs are essential (market world, Mordida) while enhancing the value/cost proposition in the thriving environments when competition is extremely high.
■ Adapt the alliance strategies according to the economic dynamics.
- Focus on increasing the number of commercial alliances with customers/peer companies in the thriving scenarios (meritocracy, market world).
- Place added emphasis on the fiduciary aspects of market relationships to stay clear of.
■ Work with government or international bodies to prevent the proliferation of corruption (Mordida) or extremely protectionist policies (managed marriage).

Lessons Learned

■ In going through this process, it was very important to keep in mind that scenario planning does not predict the future. No matter how likely one scenario appears to be, the organization must take advantage of the insights achieved to prepare for a future that would largely be a combination of two or more of the scenarios envisioned.
- The Motorola 2010 scenarios were no exception. Although there are still five more years to go on the planning horizon, we see the world situation leading up to 2010 shaping mainly as a combination of two main scenarios: meritocracy (thriving Asia) and managed marriage (thriving Europe) (see Figure 4).
■ The strategic insights resulting from the meritocracy scenario did provide the right focus to capitalize on the growth of the Asian region, especially the opportunities presented by China and Southeast Asia.
- Increased investments in the region paved the way for Motorola's strong position in this market.
- Enhanced relationships with government, customers, and sales channels provide sustainability to Motorola's businesses as they expand into the future.

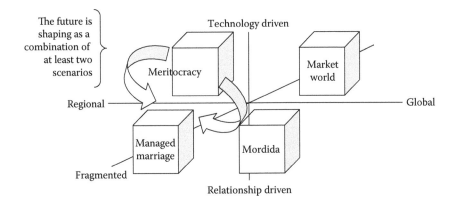

Figure 4   2010 scenarios.

■ The chief challenge that resulted from the 2010 scenario exercise was the need to drive momentum for a stronger China/Asia business throughout the company while keeping ahead of opportunities in Europe. A robust multiregion strategy has proven essential in preparing for 2010, as the vision for a unified Europe is now a reality, and the region will do what it takes to sustain and advance its power in the world economy.

Appendix: Company Background/Profile

Company name	Motorola, Inc.
Founded	1928
Business type	Global manufacturer of wireless, broadband, and automotive communications technologies and embedded electronic products. (Semiconductors were offered by the Motorola's former semiconductor sector, now a spin-off company named Freescale.)
Mission (then/now)	Transform innovative ideas into products that connect people to each other and the world around them, make things better, and life easier.
Product lines	Two-way radio solutions for public safety, government, transportation, utility, other segments Digital cable set-top terminals and cable modems Mobile phone handsets Infrastructure technology for mobile telephone service Integrated systems for autos, portable electronic devices, and industrial equipment
2004 sales	$31.3B
Business segments	Connected home solutions Government and enterprise mobility solutions Mobile devices Networks

Technology Milestones (1994–2004)

1994	World's first commercial digital radio system that integrates paging, data, voice dispatch, and wireless telephones in a single radio network and a single handset
1995	World's first two-way pager, the Tango
1996	World's smallest and lightest wearable cellular telephone, the StarTAC
2000	World's first 700-MHz wideband high-speed data trial with public safety users
2001	First metal mobile phone, the Motorola v60, with Internet access, text messaging capabilities, and voice-activated dialing; first single-chip Global Positioning System receiver solution, instant GPS chip
2003	World's first handset combining a Linux operating system and Java technology with full PDA functionality, Motorola A760 phone
2004	Ultra-slim, metal-clad, quad-band flip cell phone, the RAZR V3; unique cross-technology solution for "push-to-talk" connectivity across and between GPRS, CDMA2000 1X, and WiFi networks

References/Acknowledgments

This case study is based on an adaptation of the findings and materials generated during the development of the "Motorola Global Scenarios" in 1993.

The scenarios, analysis, and recommendations discussed for this case study are a joint product and property of Motorola and GBN. The methods and principles of scenario planning discussed in this case study were authored by GBN. Team facilitation and scenario interpretation, refinement, and documentation were outsourced to GBN.

Acknowledgment for making the scenario materials available for the case study goes to Tom Davis (Motorola, Inc.). Sources consulted during the interpretation and documentation of these scenarios included: E.F. Vogel: *Japan as Number One*; Dahrendorf: *Reflections on Eastern Europe*; Thurow: *Head to Head*; Ohmae: *Borderless World*; J.S. Nye: *Bound to Lead*; Tibbs: *Industrial Ecology*; Kotkin: *Tribes*; Tyson: *Who's Bashing Whom*; Michael Creighton: *Rising Sun*; Emmott: *The Sun Also Sets*; Kennedy: *Preparing for the Twenty-First Century*.

CI at a Major Telecommunications Company

Peter McKenney

Introduction

Competitive intelligence (CI) adds no value unless it is put to use. This case study will explore a collaborative relationship between a CI consulting firm and a Fortune 500 telecommunications corporation. This partnership has evolved over time and illustrates a unique, cost-effective method of integrating CI within a corporation. This innovative approach delivers a solid return on investment by optimizing the use of scarce resources.

Cipher Systems

Headquartered near Washington, D.C., Cipher is an international consulting firm specializing in market research and CI. The firm was established in 1996 to fill an unmet need in the marketplace for collection and analysis of business-sensitive market data. Since its inception, it has pioneered methodologies and software that enable these activities to scale across global operations.

Cipher has a presence in Asia, the Middle East, North and South America, Western Europe, and Australia. Key clients operate in the telecommunications, life sciences, chemical manufacturing, and energy industries. Cipher consultants also support the information needs of a number of federal government agencies.

With Cipher, organizations of all sizes are able to cut through the information glut and make better choices. Using unique and time-proven research methodologies, Cipher analysts collect, analyze, and report on details related to a client's markets, customers, and leading competitors. Research activities are focused around specific topics/questions and are designed to result in actionable intelligence deliverables.

Using scientific search, analysis, and reporting technologies, Cipher has also automated much of the intelligence collection process that underlies strategic decision making. The company remains at the forefront, tailoring a combination of research, analysis, and consulting services with technology tools including its award-winning software Knowledge.Works™.

Cipher helps professionals to be proactive and work more efficiently. Its solutions drive executive decisions and impact a wide range of business strategies resulting in product innovation, supply chain simplification, process modifications, and an overall increase in revenue.

Telecommunications Corporation

General Company Information

The second subject in this case study is a Fortune 500 telecommunications provider headquartered in the United States. Similar to many firms in this particular industry, the history of this corporation is the result of the merging of corporate strengths and is marked by continuous technology change.

Realizing that the Internet would create demands that existing networks could not possibly meet, this corporation set out to build a new kind of network — faster, more flexible, and more robust than any network on earth. Strategic acquisitions over time gave it a greatly expanded geographic footprint as well as a slate of advanced technologies including Digital Subscriber Line (DSL) services, advanced frame relay, and others.

Today, its network contains the world's most advanced optical networking equipment. In the United States alone, its advanced fiber-optic network links nearly 30 million customers through more than 2.6 million miles of fiber. The combination of technologies, applications, and experience moves this corporation to a place solidly among the leaders in Internet and Web services.

CI Group

The CI group is part of the market intelligence group at this corporation. Market intelligence reports to the executive vice president (EVP) of corporate communication. The EVP for corporate communication is a member of the senior management team. Consequently, the CI group is strategically positioned to provide analysis to top management on a regular basis.

The market intelligence group is comprised of three distinct workgroups: CI, market research, and database marketing. The three groups focus on specific market research areas but are also divided into cross-functional teams. The three workgroups share information on a regular basis.

The CI group is small. There are seven members whose focus is both ongoing or *tactical* and forward thinking or *strategic*. Tactically, the group is set up to monitor trends affecting the consumer and business units within the corporation's geographic area. Strategically, CI also looks at specific product innovations and changes that may impact the corporation's customer base. CI is headed by a veteran CI professional with a background in military intelligence.

The market research group is focused on customer-related research. They are primarily responsible for customer satisfaction. This group looks at trends in the industry and how they may impact the product mix that the corporation offers. The analysts conduct focus groups and other primary market research designed by the team to enhance the product mix and drive customer satisfaction. CI and market research often work together. For example, market research considers product trends, whereas CI focuses on what key competitors are offering. CI uses all of this information to analyze the potential impact to corporate strategy and the bottom line.

The database marketing group manages internal and external customer data. They are the number crunchers of the market intelligence group. Their customer data warehouse is used for sampling purposes by the market research group. For example, they use it to find areas within the corporate territory that are underserved by a technology or product mix. Then it is up to CI to analyze if the area is a good market for product introductions. In this way, the groups work together to ensure that key competitive areas are monitored.

The two major drivers of the corporation are to improve revenue as well as service. With this in mind, each of the three groups routinely shares research requests with one another. This integration between the three groups maximizes scarce human resources. It also enables each group to add their unique piece of the market intelligence equation to the overall analysis.

The market intelligence group has a high profile with senior executives. According to the CI group director, this is a good position for CI. To be effective, this function needs to be high enough in the organization to routinely interact with key executives. This is the only way to make sure that CI is focused on the right high-impact issues that really make a difference to the bottom line.

The CI group in particular interacts directly with several key executive-level workgroups. CI is structured to tactically evaluate changes in both the consumer and business core products. This information is frequently requested by various members of the senior management team. As a result, CI participates in biweekly meetings with key personnel to evaluate top threats and responses.

The CI group is also involved in product development, regulatory compliance, legal concerns, and many other areas of the business. In all cases, their efforts contribute directly to both ad hoc decision making and long-term strategy development.

The Strategic Intelligence Relationship

No matter what area of the telecommunications industry you consider — wireless, wireline, or broadband/cable — companies need to stay on top of new technologies, track and analyze competitors, and monitor their products and services. The development of new products depends on and generates new knowledge and information related to the discovery and application of these developments. A competitive or market intelligence function is imperative to aggregate and analyze the details needed to make timely, well-informed, strategic business decisions about:

- Developing, continuing, or terminating projects
- Evaluating companies that might be appropriate partners, or merger and acquisition candidates
- The competition and insight into their strengths, weaknesses, and strategies
- Identifying innovative go-to-market strategies and ways to combat the competition
- Locating experts who can assist with regulatory and public policy issues

Given the importance of the function of CI within the corporation, the director of the CI group had two key factors driving him to pursue a relationship with an outside vendor. First and most immediate, his team needed some additional resources to help respond to an increasing number of research requests. Second, he needed an independent group to conduct unbiased research. From the onset, the director was looking for a trusted partner he could rely on to do market studies quickly and with a degree of anonymity that his department alone could not achieve. Cipher was the partner he chose.

Lessons Learned

This strategic intelligence (SI) relationship was initially developed on a bid or project basis. Every request the corporation had for Cipher had to have an RFP, which included an analysis of resources needed as well as a cost analysis. The work on these RFPs was time-consuming and labor-intensive on both sides. The corporation had to devote some of its limited resources to writing up the request, and Cipher had to respond in kind. Once the bid was accepted, Cipher had to have the human resources available to complete the work in a timely manner.

As a result, valuable time was lost on the front end of projects to take care of these administrative issues, and additional costs were incurred. The time factor was also a concern as most of these projects had a very short turnaround time to begin with.

Learning from the experience they had shared working together, the two organizations took this relationship to the next level. In 2002, a contract was put in place that gave the CI group dedicated Cipher resources. The contract continues to be renewed on an annual basis and includes both planned and ad hoc research support.

Mutual Benefits

The relationship between the CI group and Cipher enables both parties to work more effectively. The CI group knows that it can depend on Cipher for help when needed, whereas Cipher has a contract in place enabling it to staff at appropriate levels. Also, because most ongoing work is negotiated annually, everyone's administrative costs go down.

Utilizing an outside research firm enables the CI group to maximize its resources. It allows the small team to focus on core analysis, strategic opportunities, and potential threats. Given the data collected by Cipher, the CI group is better positioned to monitor competitors, emerging technologies, and market activity. With the additional resources, it can guarantee timely responses to both tactical and SI requests.

The CI group also benefits in other ways more directly related to the research itself. For example, Cipher developed a mystery shopping program for the corporation. This enabled the CI group to get an independent analysis of how their products compared with the competition. It is important to note that the results of mystery shopping by an independent source typically have more validity than those generated by an internal program.

For Cipher, the ongoing contract means it is able to provide the right resources when needed by the CI group and still meet the commitments of other clients. The Cipher analysts who work with this corporation are all experts in the field of telecommunications and are highly skilled researchers. They handle the ongoing monitoring of competitors, product strengths–weaknesses–opportunities–threats (SWOT) matrices, and weekly literature scans, as well as the ad hoc research requests the CI group receives from various market groups within the corporation.

In the end, both parties benefit from the ongoing nature of the relationship. Given the long-term focus of the relationship, a high level of trust has been developed, and all expectations are clearly understood.

CI in Action: VoIP Strategy

Let us consider a specific example of the power of putting CI in action. Here, we will take a look at one specific telecommunications strategy that is being greatly impacted by the relationship between Cipher and the CI group at this corporation. This case study clearly illustrates the criticality of the decisions supported by the CI group and its influence on the senior management team.

This example is in the area of new technology adoption of Voice over Internet Protocol (VoIP). VoIP is a technology that allows an individual to make telephone calls using a broadband Internet connection instead of a regular (or analog) telephone line. VoIP represents a fundamental shift away from the circuit-based telephony architecture that has been the backbone of the telecommunications infrastructure for more than 100 years.

As with any new technology, decision makers at this corporation are all at various places on the learning curve regarding the potential of VoIP as a strategy for the company to pursue. Likewise, they are at different stages in their understanding of how VoIP will fundamentally change telecommunications as it has been offered since its inception. One thing is certain: VoIP technology and the impact it will have with competitors will fundamentally change the company. Recognizing this, the CI group pursued an aggressive strategy to educate management.

Influencing Change

Early on, the CI group recognized that the best approach to promoting an understanding of VoIP's potential was to educate management on how it could be used and applied, rather than just throwing around a lot of acronyms and technical verbiage. For example, the CI group used the analogy of the railroad to explain VoIP's potential. Using analogies and other story-telling tools can be quite effective.

A hundred years ago, the railroad was king and there were many who could not envision a world without most goods and services as well as people being transported over the rails. Automobiles had only been around a decade and airplanes were in their infancy. There were very few paved roads and no interstate highway system. The change from railroads to automobiles was gradual. One of the keys to success then as now for companies was recognizing the potential of a new technology and understanding how it could benefit an organization. Analog telephony can be equated to the railroads of a hundred years ago. VoIP is the new telecommunications method just like automobiles and airplanes replaced the railroad as dominant transportation methods. Just as railroads still exist though in a greatly reduced role, so will the telephone as we currently know it coexist with VoIP.

Although there is great potential for VoIP at this corporation, the real opportunity comes in the form of new applications. The IP network utilized can support many different formats. This requires a fundamental change in mindset for many corporate decision makers. They need to shift gears and recognize that this new technology means there will actually be less revenue coming in from traditional voice applications. Rather, the opportunity for new applications and subsequent new revenues from IP applications is unlimited. The success secret is in recognizing what applications the consumer ultimately will buy and then tailor the product mix to satisfy these requirements and generate new demand.

This is where the CI group and Cipher are already making a big impact at this corporation.

Educating through CI

A key role of the CI group at the initial stages of the adoption of new technology is to educate all levels of management within the company on the true potential of this new technology. Once the management team begins to accept this new way of thinking at a high level, it can begin to educate its staff as the new knowledge spreads throughout the organization.

The CI group is responsible for delivering the details needed to make proactive decisions in areas such as product direction. One standard delivery mechanism used by the CI group includes executive presentations. These show a thorough analysis of the technology and what the competition is doing with VoIP. They also discuss the opportunities for the corporation. Cipher is integral to this process by providing ongoing research and monitoring of the competition. This allows the CI group to continue its focus on analyzing the collected data and communicating it to key decision makers.

Understanding the Facts

As with any intelligence question, many important details come from uncovering the facts. Pulling the right pieces of data to create an accurate picture for management is another important aspect of CI. This is also a critical factor in alleviating concerns and disbelief.

The CI group estimates that VoIP will become the standard for the business market within ten years. This forecast is based on a number of key findings. For instance, Osterman Research estimates that although only about one third of organizations have deployed a VoIP system and only 10 percent of users currently employ VoIP in a workplace, it anticipates that VoIP penetration will reach 45 percent of users by late 2007, barring any significant changes to the regulatory landscape or unexpected economic shifts.

As with any new technology, a number of legitimate concerns have surfaced. It is the role of the CI group to provide the details necessary for management to fully understand the impact of these questions and review appropriate options for addressing them.

For example, one initial concern that surfaced was the belief that VoIP would cannibalize the company's other product offerings. Providing a detailed market/industry audit of the telecommunications market over the next five to ten years is therefore a critical component of the CI group's overall intelligence plan. This will illustrate what the product mix will look like in the future. It will help uncover new opportunities.

There are also prevailing concerns in the marketplace about the reliability of VoIP and the loss of existing investments in telephony technology. These are important issues for the CI group to examine as they consider recommendations for product development and marketing. To address these concerns, the lower cost of VoIP and the quality of services and products for remote users are just two highlights. In addition, the corporation has undertaken rigorous market trials of VoIP to demonstrate the reliability of its systems.

Communicating Early Warning Signals

Here, we consider just a few examples of how the CI group will need to continue to push the management team to think outside of the box. Remember, CI is not just about understanding what is happening in the marketplace today — it is about knowing what your competitors are going to do next and beating them to the punch.

The CI group needs to keep this in mind as it conducts research studies and pulls together the analysis for delivery to its management team. They can leave no stone unturned as they recognize and communicate the early warning market signals that are going to keep this corporation in its leadership position. It is Cipher's role to collect the data that they need to do this.

Consumer Adoption

Although the consumer adoption of VoIP will be slower than the business market, Information Gatekeepers, Inc., suggests that by 2010, network VoIP will be serving nearly 20,000,000 households — about 25 percent of the potential market. (Note that the potential market is defined as those households with high-speed access.) The market value analysis subsequently suggests that the network VoIP market can near a value of $1 billion by 2010. This is not something to be ignored.

Usability Issues

Currently, the technology can be cumbersome and difficult for the average consumer to use. A good analogy would be to remember back to the days when PCs were using DOS — before Windows. As soon as IP applications, whether it be voice or another application, become easier to use, the adoption rate will increase exponentially just as PCs became a necessity rather than a luxury soon after the introduction of Windows. This is something the corporation needs to take into consideration when developing its VoIP strategy. The CI group with the help of Cipher will keep them on the leading edge of this wave.

Regulatory Compliance and Legal Concerns

Although the potential for VoIP is great, there are intangibles to it as well. These intangibles include the consolidation of major carriers as well as potential legislation both at federal and state levels. These particular intangibles can, and probably will, impact the speed at which VoIP is adopted. There is no way that the intangibles will eliminate VoIP; they only have an ability to slow down the eventual adoption of various IP applications. The CI group is aware of these intangibles and, together with Cipher, monitors them as part of its ongoing work.

Conclusion

There are several different approaches to CI. Some corporations, for example, prefer a very formal, structured, and centralized approach. Others handle it through a purely ad hoc system. With the telecommunications leader considered here, the CI group has found just the right mix of internal and external resources to be successful.

The CI group is uniquely positioned in the hierarchy of the organization. It has the executive-level support and attention it needs to be successful with just a small dedicated group. In conjunction with the other components of the market intelligence group, the senior management team at this corporation has the information it needs to make solid, forward-thinking decisions.

Cipher plays an integral role in the success of the CI group at this corporation. This relationship is a cutting edge example of how to manage a complex CI function with limited human resources. This relationship enables the corporate CI group to respond quickly, efficiently, and accurately to tactical intelligence requests while also maintaining a strategic focus on trends that may impact the company or its product offerings. The relationship enables the corporate CI group to maintain its high visibility while keeping overheads to a minimum.

Bibliography

Federal Communications Commission, FCC Consumer Facts, VoIP/Internet Voice, http://ftp.fcc.gov/cgb/consumerfacts/voip.html.

Cipher Systems LLC, http://www.cipher-sys.com/.

Gartner Group, http://www.gartner.com/.

Telecommunications Corporation — Corporate Website, The name of the corporation cannot be disclosed for confidentiality reasons.

The Voice of the Lightwave: VoIP How Will VoIP Impact the Telecom Industry, Published by Information Gatekeepers, May 2004, http://www.igigroup.com/st/pages/voip.html.

Trends Section, *Communications News*, April 2005, http://www.comnews.com/stories/articles/0405/0405trends.htm.

Personal Interviews: Kathy Reese, Senior Research Analyst, Cipher Systems, Two senior members of the CI Group at the subject telecommunications corporation.

Strategic Intelligence in AARP

Shereen Remez

Introduction

In 2008, the American Association of Retired Persons (AARP) will be 50 years old. We have been called America's most powerful lobby, the biggest organization in the world (with one exception: the Catholic church), the 800-lb gorilla of organizations. One thing is certain, though. AARP is the focal point and the center of knowledge about people over 50. With nearly 36 million members, our years of polling, thousands of interviews, countless focus groups and surveys, and with hundreds of aging and policy experts on staff, AARP is the information source for and about this group. We think of ourselves as the repository for data on our constituents' attitudes, opinions, and behavior. Furthermore, we believe that if we want to continue to grow and enhance our "market share," it is important as part of our future strategy to expand our knowledge, which ultimately supports our positioning as a positive force for society.

AARP employs over 1800 staff, located in its Washington, D.C., headquarters and in 53 state offices (District of Columbia, Puerto Rico, and the Virgin Islands) across the nation. AARP's international office plays an important role in worldwide policy development concerning aging; although AARP has no official offices abroad, it does have members in Canada and Mexico.

Some might conjecture that an organization this powerful and strong has no real competitors. But they would be wrong.

Demographics alone conspire to both expand AARP's influence and to bring new competitors to the marketplace. The United States (and the developed world at large) is facing the largest demographic changes in history as the 76 million American baby boomers begin to age. The boomers, of course, were born between 1946 and 1964, with the oldest poised to hit 60, whereas the youngest are just turning 41 years of age. This puts the cohort directly in the sights of AARP, and also makes it central to the marketing and growth strategies of many other companies, such as the GAP, Chico's, Home Depot, Anheiser-Busch, Fidelity, Vanguard, and many others. Everyone is talking about how this new generation of elders will reinvent what it means to be older, and how they will continue to dominate consumer spending for decades to come. Second homes, second mortgages, second marriages, second careers, and second midlife crises, all seem to fuel the ferment and excitement around this market. Competition for the hearts, minds, and wallets of AARP membership is the inevitable result. Thus, to expand AARP's corporate agility, we have launched extensive strategies around the big three strategic drivers: knowledge management (KM), competitive intelligence (CI), and business intelligence (BI).

First, I think it is important to qualify this case study with the statement that strategic intelligence (SI) — that is, KM, BI, and CI — are journeys, not destinations. In today's competitive world, even nonprofit corporations are dealing with rapidly changing economic and social factors, a shrinking world that is marked by global trends (such as an aging workforce) and a demographic tide that is unsurpassed in history. To build a social–entrepreneurial environment requires both constant innovation and extreme discipline in execution — rare in most commercial corporations and even rarer among nonprofits.

Still, we think we are on the right track — although the destination seems to continually move toward the horizon and into the future.

Knowledge Management

KM, as a concept and as an organization, was introduced to AARP by Dawn Sweeney, currently AARP Services president and then associate executive director for membership at a time when KM was a top-notch research organization staffed by many PhDs and other social scientists. Their charge was to perform and disseminate knowledge about AARP's members and issues. Our transformation of this entity from a traditional research organization with an emphasis on the creation of knowledge (surveys, focus groups, Internet panels, etc.), to an organization with a seat "at the table" and engaged in decision support (consulting, contextual scanning, implications, and action), spanned three years.

How did this come about? As the director, I made it clear from the beginning that excellent research was baseline, not distinguishing or "value add." To move from the backroom to the boardroom, it would require every researcher to share his or her knowledge throughout the life cycle of research — from planning to execution to analyzing results to determining action. The following is a question guide that we generally followed and may be helpful in bringing a KM perspective to research in any organization.

Determining the Opportunity or the Problem

What does the client hope to accomplish with the research? What will be done with the research when it is completed? What if the answers are unexpected and not what you hoped for? Do you (the researcher) and the client (the program manager) understand the context? Will the implications and actions that result be primarily internal or external to the organization? How will you recognize (measure) success?

Developing the Team

Who should be on the team (interdisciplinary)? Are the right players at the table (legal, financial, program, research, communications, and external experts)? How often should you meet? Do you have an executive (C-level) sponsor? Who is taking the lead responsibility?

Executing the Project

Does the methodology fit the problem at hand? Are you engaging external contractors? Who is responsible for various parts of the project? Does the project timeline fit the needs of the organization? Are you executing within budget constraints? Are you frequently communicating with all relevant stakeholders through multiple channels (e-mail, telephone, Web conference, in person)?

Implications and Actions

This is the most crucial step in the process, whether the results are knowledge from research, CI, or BI.

What are the objective results (especially the "aha's!")? How do these results square with other factors you know from other sources of data, information, or knowledge (CONTEXT)? How might the organization act upon this information (innovation, problem solution, avoidance of risk, public relations or publicity [positive or avoid negative], message use [in advertising], and management improvement)?

Follow-Up

What were the results? How was the knowledge used (decision support, message testing, marketing, evaluation, etc.)? To whom was the knowledge disseminated, and what did they do with it? Were any crucial decisions made as a result? Was the client satisfied (or thrilled) or disappointed? What are the lessons learned from the project? How might the same knowledge be reused in a different way or for a different problem? Did the researcher (knowledge expert) get and maintain a "seat at the table" throughout the process? If the knowledge uncovered was ignored or doubted by management, why? What could be done better next time?

Evaluation

Did the organization achieve the metrics established to measure success of the project? To what extent did the knowledge base influence this outcome? What are the logical next steps?

In addition to completely reinventing our approach to applied research in AARP, we also built up the knowledge-sharing infrastructure. This was led by our knowledge architect, Abby Pirnie, who joined AARP after formerly serving as a chief knowledge officer. We instituted, organization-wide, three common KM tools:

The Corporate Yellow Pages

Many top-level managers and executives complained that they could not find the people they needed to talk to. For example, a senior manager might be looking for someone to help them with an issue concerning AARP's volunteers. We wanted a system that would identify the right people at the right time — for a number of uses. This was a technology project first, as AARP needed the functionality that would enable its 1800 national and state employees to "know one another" better. Second, we needed to do this in a simple and easily accessible way. We decided early on that we did not want a technology that automatically "read" e-mails and "built" a profile based upon that data. We wanted an infrastructure that was easy to use (no training required), accessible to all, and, of course, searchable.

We began with a company that hosted our information on an external server. All that participants needed to do was access the site and fill in the blanks about their names, e-mail addresses, phone numbers, etc., and write about their work experiences and skills. Once the database was completed, it became searchable, by skill, experience, or other factors. As the first pilot, I required all of my staff (around 80) to complete their pages on the Web. There was some resistance to this, but eventually nearly everyone complied.

Abby Pirnie was then ready to roll this application out to the entire organization. She began by identifying contacts throughout the organization who could serve as catalysts and "help desks," extending our reach into the organization. There was a lot of enthusiasm for the application we selected: the interface was attractive, it allowed automatic updates from our HR system of names, phone numbers, addresses, etc., and when we put a link on our internal Web site (Infonet), it was easily accessible by all.

Again, the challenges in implementing this tool were considerable. Coordination among KM, IT, and the training office (Performance and Learning Center) were crucial to success. Participation by the majority of AARP staff also was needed. Finally, updating the bios periodically was also a challenge.

AARP has an online telephone directory that contains a significant number of data fields on each employee, as well as a photograph fed automatically from our security (ID cards) database. This system is already linked to our organization charts. Connecting the corporate yellow pages to the AARP telephone directory is the final phase of the roll-out. This will enable even simpler access to the yellow pages and more integration and, therefore, more usage.

How can the AARP corporate yellow pages be used? First of all, it helps staff who want to find an expert in "multivariate analysis," Power-Point, or some other skill. Second, it can be used to form interoffice work teams. Third, it can used to identify potential candidates for job openings. Fourth, it can be used to identify people with core skills and competencies or organizational gaps in those skills (such as marketing). And the list goes on. I have used it to get to know field staff with whom I would be visiting, but had not met. New employees can explore the yellow pages to find out who is here and who knows what.

The main challenges have been: (1) selecting the right system for the organization, (2) implementing the system, (3) convincing staff that populating the database is worthwhile, and (4) continuous maintenance and upgrades and keeping the system content up-to-date.

SharePoint Services

AARP often operates in a matrix management mode, with members of the team originating from different parts of the organization, or even from outside of the organization (consultants, providers, contractors, etc.). The problem to be solved was how to enable communication and work across time and distance, and how to collect the work of the team so that it can be shared and saved.

AARP examined multiple solutions and finally settled on SharePoint, largely because we are a Microsoft environment. The license for the software was part of our site license, and the implementation and maintenance were simplified as a result of having a Microsoft infrastructure.

The functionality of SharePoint is quite robust. It includes the ability to keep track of team members, send e-mails, post meetings and notes from meetings, send important documents, to carry on threaded discussions over time, and to archive the materials for later use.

Any one SharePoint Web site can be launched quickly in a matter of days and administered decentrally by a single individual with little training. However, a site administrator is required to keep things moving.

Today, AARP has dozens of SharePoint sites, some active, some not. Some of these sites support "communities of interest" or "communities of practice."

Communities of Practice

AARP began launching communities of practice in 2001. We defined these communities as loosely organized groups who came together to share knowledge about a common interest.

The first groups focused on baby boomers (AARP's next-generation membership), editorial expertise, and rural-area issues and needs, as well as Hispanic interests. Some of the groups met periodically in person, some met exclusively by teleconference, but all had a SharePoint site to support their work.

As we mentioned in the earlier section, AARP now supports dozens of sites, and nearly as many communities of practice.

In addition to these initiatives, Abby Pirnie conducted many information and training sessions and held two organization-wide and very well-attended knowledge fairs. She also produced a DVD that outlined our KM capabilities and showcased our talents.

Competitive Intelligence

In today's complex and highly competitive environment, even nonprofits need to understand the environment they work in and the competitors they may face. It is a simple survival technique to stay one step ahead of changes that may threaten even the most successful organizations.

As part of KM's environment analysis division and its research information center (library), we have been providing some CI, scanning, and analysis reporting for the past two years. This is all proprietary information that has as its goal the increased understanding of specific trends, specific organizations, and specific opportunities or threats.

However, the level of this "hit and miss," ad hoc effort has not proved to be sufficient. As the world's most valuable demographic — the baby boomer generation — becomes age-eligible (50+) for AARP membership, we also inherit many competitors who compete for a share of our members. Other membership organizations, of course, but also buying clubs, discount travel, insurance, financial planning and investment, and health organizations — all can be seen as dealing in the same marketplace as AARP. With nearly 36 million members, it is crucial that we conduct what we call strategic analysis. A newly reinforced strategic analysis group will help AARP by providing an early warning system for potential significant events in different sectors of AARP interest. It will also provide an ongoing assessment of trends in the marketplace, conduct scenario planning and what-if analyses, and provide data that will be the basis for AARP's biennial strategic planning. It will be charged with distributing the learning and insights across the association, and for leading change toward a new "culture of analysis" and increased awareness of market factors.

We know that in most sectors, the "knowledge corporation" has the strategic advantage, and certainly strategic knowledge about the competitive environment can be a huge catalyst for growth.

Companies that fail to consider competitive factors may find themselves unpleasantly surprised by seemingly sudden changes in the market environment. For example, the Internet (Web) brought many cases of unrecognized competition in the book market (Amazon), the encyclopedia business (Britannica), and the financial investment market (Schwab). Were these Internet trends unknown or just ignored until the pain became too great?

There are three factors that characterize organizations that are prime candidates for these types of often unpleasant surprises:

1. Mature companies with very successful business formulas and track records
2. Companies who tend to be risk-averse and resistant to change
3. Companies who tend to be organized in silos or stovepipes, such that one part of the organization has no idea what another part is doing

At AARP, we are now putting a stronger emphasize on SI, environmental scanning, and identifying opportunities and threats. This will be an integral part of our biennial strategic planning process, and will become an integral part of each of our focus areas.

Business Intelligence

Our BI initiative has centered on developing organization-wide data architecture and developing a plan for member relationship management (our version of CRM). A journey, not a destination, our BI efforts have involved: building a data warehouse, outsourcing, replatforming our primary membership database, upgrading our transactional systems, and bringing together the business leaders within the organization to develop a multiyear plan and discuss needs, governance, policy, flow, and other issues that need to be resolved to maximize our BI.

Conclusion

Today's organizations, whether in the profit or nonprofit sectors, are finding that technology and data-driven analysis can really provide a tremendous competitive edge. The journey, however, is a difficult one. It requires leadership, vision, discipline, teamwork, execution, and perseverance. At AARP, we have taken many of the first steps toward building this SI infrastructure that we hope will allow us to better serve our members and society at large.

Northrop Grumman Information Technology: Business Intelligence Case Study on "Information Assurance" Competitive Analysis

Stephan Berwick

Market Leadership versus Market Knowledge

As of 2003, Northrop Grumman Information Technology (NGIT), the second-largest sector of Northrop Grumman with revenues just under $5 billion, was ranked first in the federal government information security (InfoSec) market by INPUT, a market research firm. Although NGIT staffers involved in InfoSec were well aware of the sector's capabilities in this arena, they were not fully aware of the sector's market-recognized leadership. There was also not a cohesive sense of the structure, offerings, and competitive threat posed by InfoSec competitors.

InfoSec, also known as *information assurance* (IA), is an extremely diverse market that encompasses both small and large vendors. NGIT is usually more concerned about large-scale competitors, whereas NGIT InfoSec marketers always seem to be competing against small niche firms who are pursuing the same contracts as big players, either on their own or as strategic partners of large vendors.

Thus, after INPUT released InfoSec vendor rankings, one strategic question arose: How are NGIT's competitors in the IA space leveraging their capabilities for InfoSec market gain?

Business Intelligence Anomaly?

INPUT, a leading government market research firm, is one of the few organizations that publish vendor rankings based largely on government-issued procurement data. And they were the only market research firm that published federal government InfoSec vendor rankings. This was of concern to the Business Intelligence Unit (BIU), because one of the BIU's operating policies is to always have at least two sources of information per topic. Without other published rankings, the BIU began to design its operating plan around four factors:

1. The InfoSec domain is an extremely diverse market with influential small, niche vendors who are very difficult to track.
2. Owing to its diversity and discrete nature, the InfoSec market is subject to different perceptions of market share, growth, and competitive landscape.
3. INPUT's rankings are based on the sometimes obtuse procurement data issued by the Federal Procurement Data Center — data often considered incomplete and unreliable.

Working with the newly established NGIT Information Assurance Working Group (IAWG), the BIU discovered one anomaly when analyzing INPUT's list of leading vendors. The IAWG had a different view of the competition than was suggested by INPUT's rankings. For the BIU, this was a core competitive intelligence (CI) issue. The anomaly indicated that the sector's business strategy in this domain was in dire need of quality CI.

The CI Plan

In early 2004, the BIU was given the green light by the sector executive director of business development to collect information for an analysis of

NGIT's prime InfoSec competitors. The BIU started from one simple yet potent focus: seek to answer the core question.

Comprised of only one full-time professional, the BIU developed an action plan that quickly accomplished four goals to handle what was a huge CI project:

1. **Under very stringent budget restraints**, the BIU proposed and obtained very modest funds to cover expenses related to internal or external research assistance.
2. The BIU quickly led a **consensus-building exercise** in the IAWG to formalize which competitors the BIU would collect information on.
3. The BIU **created a schematic** of the project that outlined the initial deliverable, while also specifying the sources and methods to be used.
4. The BIU analytic schematic specified that each of the **competitors be examined around NGIT's proprietary InfoSec service and product model** to provide a seamless competitive comparison for ease of CI use by the IAWG.
5. The BIU **evaluated available internal CI-applicable resources** that would be most appropriate for this CI project.

Because of the discrete nature of the InfoSec market, as well as the lack of cohesive knowledge about over a dozen competitors on whom the IAWG sought intelligence, the BIU had to establish parameters early on.

Sources and Methods

Most important, the establishment (on paper) of specific sources and methods was crucial. Emphasizing the use of open published sources was the thrust of the BIU. Anchored in inspired analysis, targeting both free and paid sources of published data was utilized for this CI initiative. Due to the sensitive nature of the InfoSec market and the large number of competitors whom the IAWG sought to understand, the BIU only utilized open sources of data — drawn from paid research subscriptions and freely available published information — to avoid any ethical pitfalls and to create a deliverable that was substantive, quotable, and ultimately usable for actionable decision making. Although the final analysis was deemed proprietary, the BIU's emphasis on open sourcing for this analysis later allowed the finished CI to enjoy wider use than just an internal document for a single strategic decision.

Building a consensus on exactly what companies to analyze was crucial for both management of the project and to best provide what the audience really needed. Over the course of two meetings and focused follow-up e-mails, the BIU focused the IAWG only on those vendors whom all agreed were NGIT's most serious competitive threats in InfoSec. This exercise brought focus to the final CI outcome, as well as an early agreement between the taskers and the providers of the CI on the deliverables that resulted.

With the final list of target competitors established and a detailed schematic to map out the project, the BIU engaged a unique internal resource to begin collecting information and provide a first-take comparative analysis. Within one of NGIT's largest business units (BUs), a team of highly trained analysts and statisticians provides sophisticated modeling and simulation to government clients. This research group (RG) included a small team of business analysts who were occasionally used by its parent BU and other NG entities to provide market research. Faced with a large-scale, comprehensive collection task, the BIU earmarked funds for this group to collect available information and provide an initial analysis that the BIU can use to produce other CI products related to InfoSec.

The RG was given circa six weeks to complete the task. Led by an analyst dedicated to competitive research, the team provided an enormous amount of data, categorized around NGIT's InfoSec product model. The data collected was drawn evenly from the sector's paid business intelligence (BI) research subscriptions services and also from data freely available online.

CI Production

The initial product from the RG was delivered in an integrated Microsoft PowerPoint file that was distributed to all members of the IAWG on CD-ROM. The file comprised of over a dozen distinct yet related presentations that covered competitors' organizational structure, certifications, service offerings, and level of partnerships. The massive product was held together by a PowerPoint master presentation, hyperlinked to the topical presentations. The IAWG members, however, found it cumbersome to maneuver and use the rich data.

Armed with this comprehensive dataset, all constructed and delivered around the original BIU schematic, the BIU was able to easily produce more refined, targeted CI of immediate business use. Four widely distributed CI deliverables were created from the RG data.

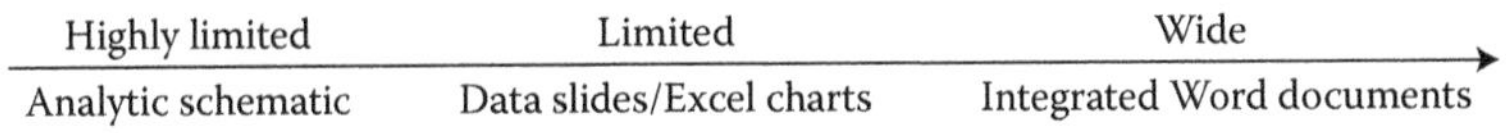

Highly limited	Limited	Wide
Analytic schematic	Data slides/Excel charts	Integrated Word documents

Figure 1 CI product distribution.

1. A ranking of the competitors analyzed based on the data categories established earlier
2. A comparative view into the level of InfoSec certifications held by the competition
3. Comparative analysis of organizational structures, based on a unique BIU analytic model
4. Detailed comparative analysis of the level of partnerships among competitors

Committing the analytic findings to paper in polished, finished forms allowed for reuse. At each step of the process, analytic findings were documented and examined at every stage of the collection and analysis. A variety of files were used, all based on the original schematic, as shown in Figure 1. With an emphasis on data presentation and analysis, CI product milestones were as follows:

1. Analytic schematic (highly limited distribution)
2. Comprehensive Microsoft PowerPoint slides, presenting both quantitiative and qualitative data (limited distribution)
3. Highly polished Microsoft Excel graphics on PowerPoint slides, presenting more refined analyses (limited distribution)
4. Microsoft Word documents integrating charts and text (wide distribution)

The BIU maintained an emphasis on product delivery for different levels of distribution throughout the CI process. This anchored the production toward increasingly refined CI deliverables of actionable impact, which in turn expanded the customer set at each stage of the process.

CI Use

These highly focused CI products were used for well over one year in both strategic and tactical contexts. The CI products were utilized in:

1. Formal strategic-level briefings
2. The corporate-wide distributed BIU monthly CI report
3. Tactical comparative profiling conducted by three BUs

The CI derived from these specific deliverables had direct impact on strategic to tactical decision making — all centered on the common theme established early in the CI process.

CI Success

Noteworthy was the BIU's success in answering the core question established at the outset. The CI initiative managed to uncover key competitive discriminators and provide a rich view into the competitive landscape of the InfoSec market. With a discernible approach to collecting targeted information and analyzing the data, the BIU was able to profile a large number of competitors in a short amount of time with highly limited resources.

CI at NGIT: The Core Question Ethos

As the cornerstone of NGIT's headquarters approach on CI, the BIU provides formal training for seasoned managers. The central theme of the training is on the importance of establishing a core question when encountering a CI task. Only from a rigorous derivation of requirements — in the form of core questions — can a CI process be targeted for business gain. The core question establishes requirements, focuses sourcing and collection, guides the final analysis, and breeds a more targeted production of CI deliverables with decision-making impact.

Transforming Data into Actionable Intelligence: Case Studies Using i2 Analyst's Notebook® and Other i2 Products

Todd Drake, Bill McGilvery, and Liza Puterman

Introduction

i2, a ChoicePoint Company, is the leading worldwide provider of visual investigative analysis software for law enforcement, intelligence, military, and Fortune 500 organizations in over 100 countries. Their integrated suite of products enables investigators and analysts to quickly understand complex scenarios and volumes of seemingly unrelated data, perform analyses, and communicate the results. For over a decade, i2's suite of software products has proven instrumental in helping organizations understand and bring clarity to complex scenarios and investigate sophisticated criminal activity. Investigative information is represented as visual elements that can be easily analyzed and interpreted. As a result, i2 products have been utilized to solve cases of fraud, drug trafficking, counterterrorism, national security, and corporate security.

Whether you need to analyze complex data, share results, organize case data, or tap existing sources of data, i2 software seamlessly provides the complete analytical solution. An individual is able to access and consolidate data from multiple sources, discover seemingly unrelated links, and apply a wide range of powerful analytical techniques. Investigators and analysts can then quickly reveal the relationships and patterns hidden within the data. They can then determine what is relevant to their investigation and assemble it into concise charts that can be easily communicated.

Analyst's Notebook® is i2's flagship software product. The software enables an analyst to create connections between people, organizations, accounts, phone records, and many other elements that are then displayed in intuitive charts. The insights gained from both link and timeline analysis can be displayed in a single hybrid analytical chart. These analytical charts are not mere visual aids. All chart items retain the information they represent on embedded data cards or through direct links to databases. This means that all source information is well organized and substantiates the charts during briefings or legal proceedings. Analyst's Notebook allows analysts to incorporate the vital element of time in any type of analysis. Analysis can be started from either a timeline or network perspective with the freedom to seamlessly switch between the two.

Analyst's Notebook can also be used by investigative agencies to share information both internally and with other cooperating organizations. Insight developed by one agency can be easily shared by simply combining charts within Analyst's Notebook. Matching entities are automatically merged, cards updated, and new links are established on the chart. The underlying data in a chart remains intact, and chart attributes can be color-coded to easily determine which agency contributed to each part of the investigation. Specific areas of the investigation can be visually divided on the chart to eliminate duplication of investigative resources. The end result is an information-sharing environment in which each organization has access to the complete intelligence picture.

Cracking an Elusive Serial Rape Case

Major investigations are carried out within law enforcement agencies by dedicated teams that include analysts, investigators, and support staff. Cases that become major investigations include high-profile murders, as well as serial and organized crimes. A major investigation can quickly become a complex maze of meaningless disparate data. i2 software assists analysts and investigators assigned to major investigations by providing the right tools that capture and organize multisource data, discover the hidden connections in the data, and communicate the results.

The Gainesville Police Department of Gainesville, Florida was in a quandary over a serial rape case. Thousands of leads were developed, leading to the difficult task of analyzing loads of seemingly unrelated data. Even as they zeroed in on a suspect, the task at hand of connecting this person to the rapes was daunting. Investigations, such as serial rape and murder cases, involve vast amounts of raw, multiformat data gathered from a wide variety of sources. Somewhere in this data lies the key to the investigation; however, that key remains obscured by the volume and apparent randomness of individual facts.

Analyst's Notebook enables investigators and analysts to turn large volumes of disparate data into actionable intelligence. The unmatched analytical power of *Analyst's Notebook* has proven to significantly increase the productivity of investigative teams, saving both time and resources. In addition, Analyst's Notebook briefing charts have proven successful in conveying complex information to superiors in an organization, and to judges and juries.

Elaine Posey, the lead crime analyst on the case who worked with the Georgia Bureau of Investigation, was tasked with analyzing the suspect's business, phone, and cash machine records to try to connect him to certain locations at certain times. As data is captured from various sources and organized, investigators need to clearly understand which pieces of information are relevant, how they relate to each other, and what it means to their case. Investigators and analysts assigned to major cases can use Analyst's Notebook to uncover hidden links in their data and focus on the most likely suspects. Analyst's Notebook is commonly used in major investigations to help: identify new investigation targets; clarify significant links, patterns, and dates; reveal the structure of a criminal organization; and produce timely information for investigative decision makers.

"As all criminal analysts know, the amount of data and information involved in an investigation such as this one is enormous," said Posey. "Without the right analysis tools at your fingertips, investigations can take a long time and often lead down the wrong path." Posey then turned to Analyst's Notebook. She imported all of the seemingly unrelated data from multiple sources into Analyst's Notebook, and within hours had created a link analysis chart that detailed all of the suspect's close associates. As a result, she was able to create a timeline chart of the suspect's actions.

The result: the suspect was eventually linked to more than 22 rape cases. "Within two weeks of using this software we had hard-core evidence against this suspect," said Posey. "Analyst's Notebook made my job easier, helping us catch a criminal much faster and creating a safer environment for the people of Georgia and Florida. There is no better feeling as a crime analyst." When it is time to obtain an arrest warrant or conviction, a "picture" linked to all the supporting evidence is worth its weight in gold.

Securing the European Football Championship

As the United Kingdom prepared to host the European Football (Soccer) Championship, the British government was determined that the sporting event would not be overshadowed by hooliganism. A special unit was set up at New Scotland Yard to police the competition. The unit included an intelligence cell equipped with i2's Analyst's Notebook, which was linked to an intelligence database. The majority of countries represented in the European Football Championship already used i2's Analyst's Notebook to combat crime in their own countries. Therefore, when each country sent a representative to liaise with the British police, the software provided a common format for exchanging intelligence. The analysts assigned to the intelligence cell used Analyst's Notebook to create charts identifying the troublemakers and the relationships between them.

The charts created by the analysts were included within the intelligence briefing packs and distributed to the operational units. The charts were used in briefings at all levels to show the remarkably complex associations identified by the analysts. Senior officers were then able to identify possible problems and prevent violent acts by targeting resources in the right locations. The charts proved to be a very powerful method of showing problem areas and significantly contributed to the success of the operation. The disruptive elements were often intercepted before they reached the stadium. The countrywide operation successfully identified and prevented many potential incidents in the days leading up to the European Football Championship. The operational teams used the intelligence to good effect, ensuring that the games were enjoyed in the trouble-free atmosphere they deserved.

Uncovering Prescription Drug Diversion Fraud

Richard Easton, a medical investigator with Forensics Intelligence Display and Analysis in Norfolk, Virginia, was hired by a defense lawyer to determine the strength of a civil suit against his client. The defendant had been accused of assaulting a postal clerk, yet the victim's injuries and credibility seemed dubious at best. Easton set out to tie together evidence proving there had been no assault.

What looked on the surface like a simple assault case turned into something much more difficult for the postal clerk to swallow; a case of prescription drug diversion. Prescription drug diversion involves fraudulently obtaining prescription drugs under the guise of treatment for a claimed injury. Typically the diverter claims a soft tissue injury, which is difficult for a physician to challenge. The pain medication prescriptions are then diverted to others and not used to treat the person alleging a need for them. The prescriptions are usually paid for by the claimant's

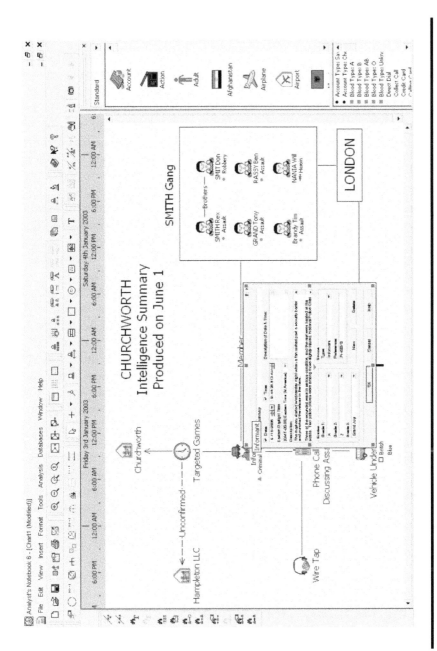

Figure 1   Churchworth intelligence summary.

insurance coverage. As a result, the person diverting the drugs spends almost no money getting the prescriptions and can sell them on the street for a hefty profit.

As Easton began piecing together medical claim information on the accuser, a blatant abuse of the prescription drug system became clear. "Utilizing i2's software, the data showed repeated, systematic visitation to different combinations of physicians and pharmacies, in different cities, with the purpose of obtaining multiple prescriptions for narcotics and other medications," said Easton. The prescriptions, with enough pills in each bottle to last for 30 days at a time, were displayed on a timeline developed with i2's Analyst's Notebook. The timeline demonstrated how the visits to physicians and resulting prescriptions overlapped time after time. The analytical charts also showed that a new visit to a new physician would result, in almost every instance, in a prescription being filled at a new or different pharmacy. "This case involved several indicators of fraudulent activity, and the analytical charts offered the ability to transform the list of chronological indicators into a display of obviously related, serial, repetitious events that were intuitively obvious to even the most casual observer that there were felonious activities in progress," said Easton.

After Easton presented the accuser's attorney with the evidence using the Analyst's Notebook timeline, the attorney realized that the simple assault was a much bigger matter than he had thought, and he dropped the lawsuit. Easton saved the defendant from going to court and uncovered a serious drug diversion case that could then be easily prosecuted. "Using i2's software, investigators can clearly present what happened in a case without having to provide an expert opinion — the charts speak for themselves," said Easton. "This software is invaluable in cases involving large amounts of seemingly unrelated data that must be pieced together to find the criminal activity."

Details of one section of the timeline show the case events clearly. Each event is a new prescription, the red lines indicating the duration of time the prescription would have lasted if the pills were taken as directed. If you draw a vertical line through the various parts of the chart, you can see how that line will cut across multiple horizontal red (duration-of-use) lines, indicating that the person had two or more prescriptions in excess of what a normal patient would need to treat a real pain in a legitimate fashion.

Analyzing High-Risk Homicide and Missing-Persons Cases

The Royal Canadian Mounted Police (RCMP) initiated a project to identify and analyze all high-risk missing persons and unsolved homicide cases

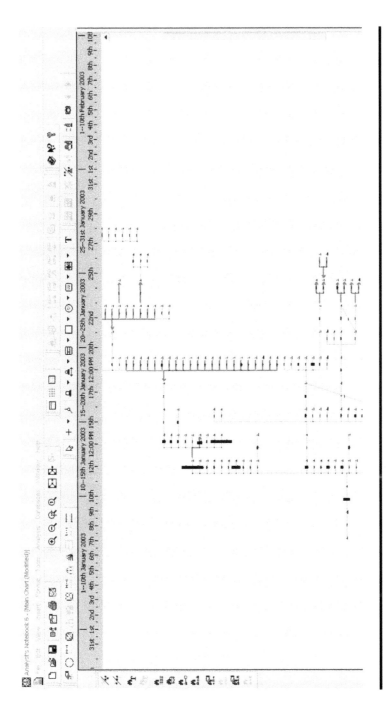

Figure 2 Example of the Analyst's Notebook timeline.

in Alberta, Saskatchewan, and Manitoba. Their goal was to determine if any cases were "potentially linked" and, if possible, to identify offenders. The High Risk Missing Persons Project (HRMPP) was a joint effort between the RCMP and the western Canadian municipal police services of Edmonton, Calgary, Regina, Saskatoon, Prince Albert, and Winnipeg. The project used a phased approach to collect, collate, and analyze thousands of current and historical police records from a variety of police information systems and from files stored in paper format — some of them decades old. The project's strategy aimed to identify persons, locations, and vehicles that existed in more than one case file. Potential "duplicates" were to be flagged for further analysis and follow-up. The principal challenge with duplicate records was organizing and formatting data such that a technology-based solution could be deployed to identify and analyze these records.

Faced with this information management task, Cpl. Brad Siddell of the RCMP, the project's information manager, approached Trinus Technologies, Inc. The firm had proven experience working with RCMP and police information systems on past projects, including the 2002 G8 Summit Security Joint Intelligence Group. Trinus, a certified i2 Partner, selected i2's Analyst's Notebook to establish any connections from the project data.

However, a method was needed to rapidly chart all records from multiple files in Analyst's Notebook. One solution could have been to perform manual imports from the case files, but Trinus were looking for a more dynamic solution. Trinus chose i2 *iBridge* to connect directly to investigation data tables. The live connection to databases via iBridge allowed analysts to expand and explore on entities in search of relevant investigation data. Trinus developed a custom plug-in that allowed i2 iBridge to connect to the project's non-native databases — much of the information was stored in tables hosted on Borland's® Interbase data engine that is not directly supported by iBridge. One of the important features of the plug-in enabled users to concurrently open multiple connections to several databases using one iBridge configuration file. Trinus was able to standardize a single iBridge configuration file to perform all search functions saving operators hundreds of hours and simplifying the technical support of the project.

While the iBridge solution was being developed and tested, Cpl. Siddell directed a team of ten data entry personnel to convert paper-based investigation files into electronic format. This task provided its own challenges, as many files were located in cities and towns some distance from any project office. To assist with this process, Trinus Technologies developed a simple data entry tool that could be used in remote locations. Once entered, simple text files were bulk-imported into a database at the project office using a Trinus-developed import utility. Tens of thousands of records were converted. Remarkably, it was the first time any attempt had been made to convert paper-based "cold cases" to electronic format.

The final major information management hurdle was to address records from other police data sources. Although these sources contained a wealth of information, much of it was stored in legacy mainframe systems. Technology issues aside, the laws that govern the release and use of this information prevented a direct connection with i2 iBridge. To overcome this challenge, a bulk record dump was requested from the host agency that was suitably vetted. Trinus Technologies then customized an import routine that placed the records directly into a compatible database at the project office.

Analyzing the multiple databases of these data-gathering efforts using iBridge resulted in 1146 person matches. These duplicates were further analyzed and, in some cases, investigated to eliminate legitimate occurrences (for example, it would be natural that a police officer's name appears in more than one case). The key finding of the HRMPP, according to the final report, was that: "A combined analysis has been conducted on 82 cases." The analysis was categorized on the basis of unsolved homicides and missing persons reports. Both of these categories included victims whose lifestyle, behavior, profession, or circumstances placed them at high risk to be a victim of violent crime.

One of the most significant achievements or findings of the HRMPP was the potential linkage of what was labeled the "priority five cases," five suspicious deaths in the Edmonton area, Alberta, that were thought to be connected. The results of the HRMPP were summarized in the executive report: "The accomplishments of the High Risk Missing Persons Project are significant. All cases identified that met the selection criteria and were included in the Phase Two analysis portion of the project were examined. Due to the HRMPP analysis, a serial offender was recognized and believed responsible for five of the criteria cases." Cpl. Siddell went on to say that: "As a result of the cross comparison of PERSON (records) between these investigations (using i2 iBridge and the plug-in), 1146 person matches were identified. Without i2 iBridge, there was no other method available to the RCMP to efficiently check for duplicates." From an information management perspective, the significance was not that duplicates were found, but the speed and efficiency with which they were identified and addressed. i2 iBridge and i2 Analyst's Notebook accomplished in days what could have taken many weeks to perform.

The final report contained over 200 i2 Analyst's Notebook charts that were generated with i2 iBridge. When combined with over 30,000 pages of database record reports, the final product became one of the most comprehensive, portable, and searchable record stores on major crimes in western Canada. The joint management team responsible for the oversight of the project has labeled the HRMPP initiative a complete success. Aside from the operational success of the project, there are significant technical benefits that will carry forward to future projects. The iBridge plug-in is already being used on other high-profile investigations, and its success has sparked further interest in a national iBridge solution for the RCMP. The HRMPP demonstrates that applying sophisticated charting technology in new and innovative ways can greatly improve the quality and efficiency of complex investigations.

Conducting Commercial Fraud Analysis

Fraud investigators must first organize all the investigative data captured from disparate sources. i2's *iBase* can be used to easily create a database that organizes and manages all the information received during an investigation, including victims and potential suspects, connection details between signatories and accounts, results of company searches, locations and addresses, and transactions for financial analyses. Because iBase can be populated quickly and easily adapted for all types of data, the database grows with the investigation. iBase includes full query and reporting capabilities and allows appropriate access to information by all members of a fraud investigation team.

Once information is captured and organized, fraud investigators need to clearly understand which pieces of information are relevant and how they relate to each other. Fraud investigators can use Analyst's Notebook to uncover hidden links in their data and focus their investigation. Analyst's Notebook techniques such as link and timeline analyses can be used to build a picture of the people, organizations, and events involved in any type of fraud investigation.

As the relationships between companies, individuals, accounts, and numerous transactions are uncovered, the working charts grow in complexity. Investigators can then focus on individual aspects of their case, producing simplified charts that cut to the heart of the case. From the start of the investigation, investigators can record the details of all source documents either on cards behind each chart element or through a direct link to a database. This ensures that when the legal process begins, all documentary evidence is organized, and it substantiates the charts. These charts are used as visual briefing aides that have proven effective in communicating complex cases to team members, prosecutors, and juries.

To more closely examine the actions of fraud suspects, investigators can use Analyst's Notebook to develop timeline charts that identify the precise sequence of case-related events. All the details from the beginning events to the apprehension of suspects are depicted in this format.

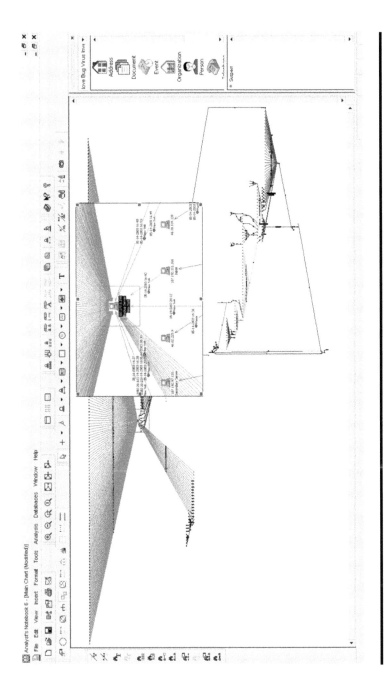

Figure 3 Example of a chart generated with i2 iBridge.

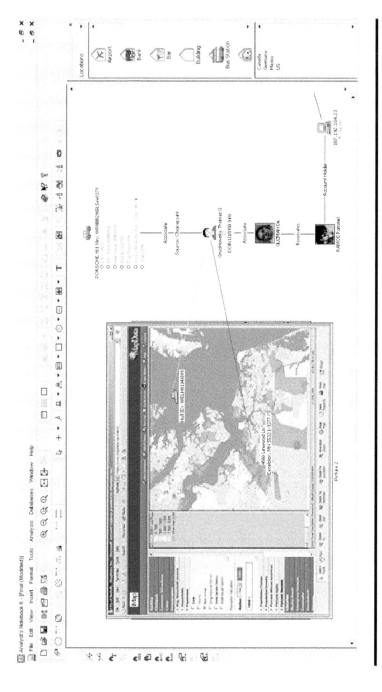

Figure 4   Analyst's Notebook screenshot.

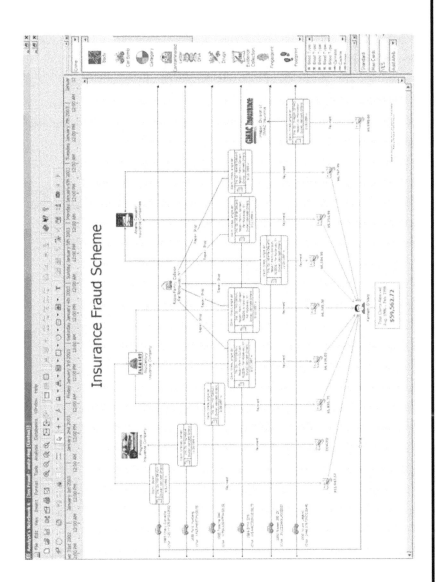

Figure 5 Screenshot of Analyst's Notebook used to create a timeline representing the precise sequence of activities.

Timeline analysis helps fraud investigators effectively communicate the timing of case-related events and can be used to summarize the investigation. As with link charts, each event on the timeline chart includes a reference to its source document or a direct link to a database.

Sophisticated white-collar criminals often go to great lengths to hide their crimes. Tracking down money, goods, or other assets fraudulently obtained can be the most challenging part of an investigation. Analyst's Notebook and iBase can be used to meticulously organize and analyze thousands of case-related transactions. Transaction analysis charts can be generated automatically from iBase or other structured data sources such as spreadsheets. Investigators find these charts invaluable in identifying repeating patterns in the transfer of money between accounts, revealing the mechanisms used by fraud perpetrators.

i2 products have proven to be the leading analytical tool in combating fraud in the commercial sector worldwide. The software has been utilized in both short-term tactical operations and long-term strategic-planning initiatives. Allied with an organization's analytical skills, i2 software has proven to enhance an organization's capabilities and lead to more informed decision making, thereby enabling one to address issues more effectively.

Surviving and Thriving Despite the Loss of a Major Customer at The Analysis Corporation

Keith B. Johnston and Clint Gauvin

Introduction

The Analysis Corporation (TAC) was faced with the unexpected and near-term loss of their largest contract. As this contract represented over 80 percent of TAC's revenue, loss of this contract threatened its ability to continue as a viable business. Although a short-term solution to this problem was found, it was necessary to get more business to replace this contract. Through the use of business and competitive intelligence and leveraging of specialized knowledge, TAC was able to turn this threat into an advantage and expand its customer base.

Background

In 2003, the mission of TAC's largest customer — a government organization* — was being transferred to two other agencies (referred to as

Agency A and Agency B). TAC's only large contract was to provide support for this mission by developing and maintaining an information system and providing mission support staff (analysts). Both of the new agencies had existing contractor relationships that they intended to use to support this mission. Although TAC had supported this customer for over 13 years and had received multiple commendations on its performance from the highest levels in the department, its relations with the people in the two organizations taking over this mission were either nonexistent or bordered on hostile. It appeared difficult for TAC to be able to continue the work they had been doing for the original organization. TAC was in a market niche that had expanded dramatically and had attracted a number of competitors, many of them much larger than TAC. Strategic intelligence also showed that TAC was in danger of being pushed aside by these larger, less experienced companies.

The only real strength TAC could muster in trying to obtain a contract with one or both of the new organizations was in the subject matter expertise and knowledge of both its mission staff (located at the government site) and systems staff (located primarily at TAC's site). Although the staff was a mixture of long-time employees and more recent hires, TAC had always made it a point to hire people who were dedicated to supporting this particular mission and were willing to work hard, and to learn what was needed to excel at their jobs. TAC supported the new staff with mission- and system-specific training, and extensive documentation, which was continually updated and improved. Although no sophisticated knowledge management system was used, new employees and employees awaiting contract reassignment were expected to use the existing training resources and systems, and make a meaningful contribution to these resources. Over time, these resources became quite well developed and comprehensive. Before new employees were sent to the government site, they had several weeks of training on the system and mentoring from more experienced analysts. At the government site, the TAC staff worked closely with people from both inside the government organization and outside of it, forming relationships that were needed to effectively perform the interagency coordination that was a big part of their job. As is now common in federal agencies, most of the institutional knowledge on this mission resided with TAC staff, and much of that was captured in the training materials.

---

* The government organizations involved would not permit use of their names in this case. Details on the organization's mission and the identity of people not affiliated with The Analysis Corporation are omitted or changed to allow them to remain anonymous.

Agency A had been involved in early planning for the reorganization and was familiar with the role that TAC staff played in accomplishing the mission. After initially determining that they would use one of their existing systems to support the part of the mission that they had inherited, Agency A eventually determined that the system at the original organization should be "cloned" and moved to their organization for temporary use until their contractor could build a replacement system. They also recognized the need to retain the expertise and institutional knowledge of TAC's mission staff. This they accomplished by issuing a contract to TAC for providing mission support personnel and delivering and maintaining a clone of the existing system.

Agency B was much more rushed in planning to accept their part of the mission. Shortly before Agency A issued their contract, Agency B realized that they would have none of the existing expertise needed to fulfill their part of the mission. They were able to negotiate with Agency A that half of the mission staff from TAC would work at Agency B to support their part of the mission, and this work would be covered for one year under Agency A's contract. The existing on-site support staff was divided according to specialty, experience, and desired career goals to best leverage the mission with the proper people in support of each organization. However, none of TAC's system staff would be provided to Agency B.

After the contract was awarded, TAC delivered the cloned system to Agency A on time. The deadlines had been very tight, so the agency was pleasantly surprised. The agency was also very pleased with the TAC analysts they got. These analysts were able to quickly integrate into the new organization, and the mission did not suffer a single day of downtime due to the reorganization. Because of the high level of performance of the TAC staff in relation to their existing mission staff contractors, TAC was soon asked to provide additional analysts to Agency A. This represented a major turnaround in relations with the customer.

Although TAC had survived loss of its biggest contract, the new contract was only a temporary reprieve. There were still a number of problems that, if not solved, would lead to a loss of staff and revenue within a year or two. The first problem was that Agency A still planned to quickly replace the system built and supported by TAC, and they intended to use their existing contractor to perform most of this work. The TAC staff would be primarily used as subject matter experts. Agency A's contractor was a much larger company that had many years of experience with Agency A. It was also not really interested in dealing with a small company that was operating under a separate contract. Employees of the existing contractor took advantage of many opportunities to disparage TAC's system and, by inference, TAC's competence in systems. Although TAC had done many projects involving cutting-edge technology and had staff who were competent in these technologies, the system used to support this mission was composed of relatively old technology. The main reason for this lag in technology was many years of budget restrictions imposed on TAC's original customer. Only the most critical changes could be made to the system, and the rest of their money was spent on small expansions of the mission staff.

These conditions meant there were multiple problems for TAC. The first of these was that TAC was unlikely to be able to expand its systems staff at this agency because they were not seen as having the technical skills to perform the work. The expectation was that as soon as the new system was ready, the TAC technical staff would no longer be needed. Another problem was that TAC's technical staff found the environment to be hostile when working with the other contractor's staff. These problems combined to make it hard to motivate and retain technical staff, because their peers treated them poorly, and they saw no future in their work. If nothing were to be done, TAC would not have any technical staff left. Although TAC continued to expand mission staff at Agency A, expansion of technical staff would be at best a longer-term opportunity. Another customer was needed for TAC to retain its technical staff.

Initial Opportunities at Agency B

As at Agency A, TAC's mission staff quickly proved their value to Agency B. Their knowledge of the mission and their established relationships made them extremely valuable sources of information, and even the most senior officials responsible for implementing the mission at Agency B often sought them out for advice.

Agency B had also decided to build a new system to support their part of the mission. To do this, they used contractors already in place for their other components. This system needed to exchange data with the TAC-provided system at Agency A. The functions to be implemented in the Agency B system already existed in the Agency A system. (Both parts of the mission had been supported by TAC's system at the original government organization.) This system needed to be operational as soon as this part of the mission was transferred to Agency B. Developing a robust, fully functional system from the ground up in less than a month was not possible, so Agency B made arrangements to share the TAC-maintained system at Agency A. Although coordination of data changes caused some problems between the two agencies, both were able to use Agency A's system to do their work. Neither agency was pleased with the arrangement because both intended to build their own systems, but the mission necessitated this.

There were numerous delays in the development of the Agency B system. In passing on competitive intelligence, TAC's staff at Agency B was reporting that there was a good deal of discontent with the contractors performing the work. They had only been able to deliver underpowered, minimally functional systems. Not only had the contractors failed to deliver the larger, newer system on time, but some were claiming the system they were developing to be proprietary property of their company. The agency was quite unhappy with the perceived attempt to hold them hostage, and they were not happy with the failure to meet the schedule. TAC's mission staff saw this as an opportunity for TAC system staff to support Agency B. They kept TAC management aware of these developments and discussed with several Agency B managers the possibility of TAC being able to help them. (TAC's mission staff was careful not to reveal any potentially confidential information, but they were able convey opinions and operational problems that were well known to most people working at the site.) Although the agency managers very much liked TAC's mission staff, they were not open to using TAC staff for their systems. A lot of time and money had been invested in the system being developed, and they looked for ways to work under their existing contracts to get the work done. As with any large or expensive undertaking, it was not (or so it seemed) in their best interests to simply write off the project. The unfortunate truth was that the existing system would simply not be mission capable within the desired timeframe. The situation was compounded by the political temperature in which the agency was operating and the pressure under which they were put to succeed.

These problems stretched out over months. Once again, TAC's mission staff talked with their government managers, offering that TAC could again "clone" their system, make minor changes needed by Agency B, and quickly meet the needs of the agency. Agency B managers were still skeptical, but they agreed to speak to TAC about how this could be done and how much it would cost. Agency A was planning to shut down the system they were sharing as soon as their new system was ready. There was also a lot of tension between Agency A and Agency B — some of it about sharing Agency A's system, and some about the information it contained — so Agency B was highly motivated to find a way to get their own system.

Despite being motivated to get their own system, they were not entirely convinced that they should ask TAC to build them the system. They still saw their ultimate system as the one that was being developed, and any other system that they would get was viewed as a short-term, stopgap system. They did not want to spend a lot of money on a system that would not be around for a long time. TAC mission staff was well aware of the needs, constraints, and sensitivities of the agency staff. They were able to brief TAC management on the government viewpoint. They identified three major areas that were potential deal breakers: cost, time to implement (both in minimizing the time and meeting the schedule), and proprietary code. Each of these areas needed to be addressed very carefully. TAC was quite willing to give the government as good a deal as possible to show what they could do. TAC was able to get an idea of the competitor's costs by comparing GSA schedule rates for similar skills and by comparisons of salaries offered to staff at job fairs. TAC knew it had low rates and believed it could offer a cost effective system because much of the needed programming was already in its existing program. It would cost a relatively small amount to make the needed changes, and the system could be completed, tested, and installed in about six weeks. Having already accomplished this for Agency A successfully, TAC was quite confident of the costs and time schedule. The issue of proprietary program code was also not seen as a big obstacle. Most of the code had been developed at government expense and was already owned by the government. A couple of components had been developed years earlier, using only company funds, so no source code would be delivered for that particular functionality. These components were licensed to the government for a minimal charge, and no source code was needed to incorporate them into the system. TAC put together a proposal that defined the system and the work to be done, and addressed each of the sensitive areas in a way thought to be seen as responding to the government's concerns.

Negotiations to build this system were rough. As predicted by the mission staff, each of the three problem areas did arise in the negotiations. Despite being prepared to address these issues, TAC negotiators were caught a little off guard by Agency's B's initial cost position — they wanted the system at little more than the cost of the hardware and the third-party software licenses. In several rounds of discussions and consultation with the TAC staff on site with the agency, it became clear where this position arose. This agency did not have a systems staff, and their mission managers assumed that installing, modifying, and configuring a large, custom-built, multiuser system should be as quick and easy as installing software on a PC — just copy files from a CD. They also objected to including any funds to cover system modifications that TAC felt would inevitably be requested as the system was being implemented. The government negotiators were finally convinced that it would cost some money and take more time than they had originally anticipated. They were still unwilling to provide any funds for unanticipated changes. Eventually an agreement was reached for TAC to deliver a system virtually identical to that of the system at Agency A. A modification to the Agency A contract was made to allow this work to be done for Agency B.

Although TAC staff was happy to get this opportunity to show how well they could execute the task, it still did not provide the long-term security needed for TAC to grow as a successful business. It also presented great risks because the agency managers were extraordinarily sensitive to cost and schedule on account of the negative experiences with their previous contractors. TAC would be held to an even higher standard than the other contractors and scrutinized according to their ability to meet timelines and customer demands with accuracy.

TAC did deliver the system on time, although slightly later than originally projected. As the installation progressed, the government managers began to make changes to the system requirements. Their mission was constantly growing and changing, and, as a result, they recognized the need for additional functionality in their disposable stopgap system. TAC technical and management staff needed to work very closely to handle communications of these issues with the agency managers. When misunderstandings arose, TAC mission staff was able to communicate the government's viewpoint to TAC, and TAC managers were better able to address the issues before they became too large. The task was eventually modified to include the additional work and slightly extend the schedule to allow the changes to be made.

Follow-On Opportunities at Agency B

TAC staff knew the importance of the work for TAC's reputation and potential additional work at Agency B. Not only was the technical work done on time and on budget, but the TAC technical staff was also able to meet with the Agency B staff and show them that they also understood the mission and their needs and show the company's vested interest in serving their mission. Every effort was made to demonstrate TAC's desire to work with the customer and the tremendous value that TAC mission and development staff brought to them. Meanwhile, relations between the agency and their other systems development contractors did not improve. It soon became clear that the "next-generation" system they had been working on would need to be implemented by another company. During the implementation of the clone system, TAC staff would frequently mention to their government contacts that TAC would love to be considered for the new system. The usual response was to wait until the clone system was operational and supported, and then it would be considered.

One of the most valuable areas in which the TAC mission staff was able to help was in the understanding of the government stakeholders and decision makers at the agency. Just as the agency's mission was evolving, so was the staff. As the agency management ramped up, the number of people involved in the systems area grew. Each one who came in brought different experiences and preferred methods. Both the mission staff and the technical staff were able to work with the new people to help explain the background and details of the mission and systems. When information of the "hot buttons" and preferred approaches of the new people became clear, the on-site staff would pass this information back to their TAC managers to make sure that TAC would know how to work best with them.

After delivery of the cloned system, TAC management felt the time was right to put together a plan to get the contract for the new system. The first step was to meet with the customer to propose a method for addressing their system needs. If this was well received, TAC would send the agency an unsolicited proposal and would work with the agency to find a contract vehicle. As planned, TAC developed and presented to the management and systems staff at Agency B a plan to implement their desired system using an evolutionary approach to systems development. The plan addressed the most critical issues that the agency had and made a case for TAC as the best company to do this work. It emphasized understanding of the mission, TAC's successful experience at Agency B, a long history of experience at its previous customer, and an approach that minimized risks posed by system changes. The plan was well received, so an unsolicited proposal was prepared and presented to the customer. Shortly after this proposal was delivered, a new information systems director was appointed at the agency. Decisions about additional work would now be his responsibility. At about the same time, TAC mission staff reported that one of the other contractors at the agency had also presented an unsolicited proposal to do the same work. This was a very large company that was well known as a strong competitor.

More bad news came from the TAC mission staff. The new IS director thought that only a large and experienced company would be able to manage development of their systems. He had invited the largest companies in the systems development and integration arena to come in to talk with him. He had heard good things about TAC but was not inclined to put a politically sensitive, highly visible systems development project in the hands of a 75-person company.

TAC could not afford to lose this opportunity. Although the IS director was not interested in interviewing TAC about building the system, except as a potential subcontractor to a larger company, TAC did have access to him because there were ongoing modifications and maintenance activities on the clone system. Every opportunity was taken to demonstrate understanding of the agency's needs and TAC's ability to perform the needed work on time and on budget. TAC's knowledge of the systems at Agency A was also helpful, because this was one of the major systems with which Agency B needed to exchange data.

TAC's performance at this agency won it a lot of allies. TAC's staff understood the mission and were able to assist others in learning their new jobs. Many of the people they helped at the agency, including agency staff and other contractors' staff, were willing to help make the connections to key players and put in a recommendation for TAC. This gave TAC staff access to people making key decisions on the direction of the agency and made TAC even more valuable in understanding the mission. It also allowed TAC to be more responsive to agency needs as they evolved.

One of the factors always uppermost in the agency managers' minds was time. They were being pressed to have systems that supported their mission and were given unreasonable deadlines. They were also in a position in which their mission was expanding and changing, leading to changes in their systems requirements. Time was one area where TAC had an advantage over their competitors, and they moved to press this advantage. Government contracting is a long, delay-filled process. For the agency to conduct a competitive proposal for the project, they would need to allow for at least six to nine months before they would have a contract. They did not have this time. A number of new, critical modifications were needed to the system. TAC presented a proposal to make these changes, and the IS director requested that another modification be made to the task on the Agency A contract to allow these system modifications to be made. TAC had another opportunity to show critical personnel that it could do the work.

The modifications required to the system were fairly complex, and required changes to interfaces with several outside agency systems. One of TAC's areas of expertise was in understanding the flows of data between the various agencies involved in this mission. TAC had small contingents of mission staff at many of these agencies and had been at the nexus of much of this data exchange for many years. TAC had documented this information, and it was available to TAC's systems architects. Because of this knowledge, TAC technical staff were able to succinctly define the needed changes, the impact of these changes, and suggest an orderly implementation plan for these changes in a single meeting with the IS director and his technical staff. This was a turning point in the thinking of the IS director. The other companies who had previously been working on the system had not really progressed significantly past the requirements stage. It became apparent that there was no other company — regardless of size — that would have the subject matter expertise and the track record that this agency needed to implement the system quickly. This view was shared by most, if not all, of the agency's management. The IS director still believed that at a future date he would need to bring in a larger company to manage the work, but saw that TAC was the best choice for the near-term work.

In looking for ways to quickly get this work under contract, the best option appeared to be a combination of modifying the Agency A contract to add more money for the short term, while working to get a separate GSA contract in place as fast as possible. There were no problems adding some additional funds to the Agency A contract, but Agency A wanted to avoid being responsible for a long-term commitment to managing a contract for Agency B. Agency B quickly set about getting their technical and contracting staff to work on a request for proposal (RFP). They requested the contracting officer prepare the paperwork for a nine-month contract. The contracting officer suggested that they give themselves more flexibility in case their planned follow-on contract took longer than expected. She suggested that they make the contract a one-year contract, with up to four option years. That way, they could have a contract in place no matter how long the wait was, and it would give them the opportunity to keep the TAC contract if they were happy with the performance. The management of Agency B was reluctant, but did agree that this was a low-risk way to handle the contract. They still intended to bring in a larger contractor as quickly as the contracting process would permit.

While working on the business issues behind the contract, Agency B technical staff was also drafting the statement of work for the RFP. In meetings between the agency's IS director and TAC technical staff, a number of questions came up on related work and technical approaches. The IS director was quite experienced in systems development and wanted to make sure that the technical approach to be used was consistent with methods he had found successful in the past. To answer these questions, TAC staff retrieved the document with the presentation made prior to the unsolicited proposal. After reviewing its contents with the IS director, he asked why he had not been shown this earlier — the approach was exactly what he wanted. (This was somewhat ironic, because he did have the presentation earlier — he just did not think it was worth looking at.) The approach presented was an evolutionary one that would replace the older system component by component with a new system using newer technologies and more functionality as opposed to replacing the entire system in one "big bang" change. The cost and schedule for these smaller changes could be more easily predicted, and the approach permitted changes in the system requirements as it evolved. Instead of producing only requirements documents, as had happened with the previous contractor, system deliveries would be made frequently, and progress would be easy to measure. Past experiences with similar systems were also given.

The IS director liked what he saw, and he decided to put all of their planned systems work into the RFP. Where he had been reluctant to consider a longer contract for TAC initially, he began to see that it may be to the agency's advantage to keep that option open.

The RFP was issued as a sole source procurement. TAC was asked to respond with a proposal in less than a week. The proposal team believed that if they were able to respond in such a way that addressed all of the agency's concerns, they may be able to get them to reconsider looking for a larger contractor. Many of their technical concerns had been addressed already, but they obviously still had some reservations. TAC's on-site staff supplied the final information needed to allay their concerns. Although the original contractors were not well thought of, some of their employees were well regarded and had built up useful experience in the year that they had been there. The agency was worried that TAC would not want to work with the other contractors.

TAC wrote its proposal in a way that amplified the approach that the IS director had liked. The proposal also contained an extensive section on how TAC would work closely with subcontractors and other experts identified by the agency. This section emphasized how TAC would integrate these people into its teams and create an environment in which the employee's company affiliation did not matter. The lessons learned by the TAC technical staff working in an environment in which they were not a real part of the team (at Agency A) actually helped in putting together details for this section. TAC could speak with authority on the types of actions that it would not do.

The proposal was submitted on time, and the agency had three days to evaluate it. When the evaluations came in, it was clear that the proposal had hit the mark exactly. The proposal had been accepted, and the debriefing on the proposal was completely positive. The information on the inclusion of the preferred employees from other companies had been correct, and it had the desired effect. The agency stated they would be quite comfortable to stop thinking about bringing in a larger contractor, because they could get all they needed from TAC.

A Methodology for Strategic Intelligence: A Roadmap Model, a Knowledge-Based Tool, and a Bio-MEMS Case Study

Francisco J. Cantu, Silvia P. Mora, Aldo Díaz,
Héctor Ceballos, Sergio O. Martínez, and
Daniel R. Jiménez

Introduction

Strategic intelligence (SI) has become an indispensable task for competitiveness and enterprise development in the modern economy. Defined as the synergy among business intelligence (BI), competitive intelligence (CI), and knowledge management (KM) for improving the organization's strategic decision-making ability, SI offers decision makers a repertoire of methods, tools, and best practices for these three areas for accomplishing the company's objectives. From the BI standpoint, as new business opportunities arise because of technological innovations or due to population growth and the globalization phenomenon, it is essential to introduce new products in the market at the right time, which keeps the company at a leading role. In the CI side, as the markets change and offer new opportunities, new competitors emerge, making it more difficult for companies that use traditional methods to keep market shares, to stay in business, and to remain competitive. Knowing what is happening and having a clear idea of its own business niches and core competencies are crucial necessities for most companies. On the other hand, a company must develop and keep a record of its own capabilities and core competencies. This requires the development of an inventory of its own resources such as financial statements, production capacities, intellectual capital, product characteristics, clients, suppliers, etc. Companies have developed corporate memories, enterprise resource planning systems (ERPs), information systems, KM systems, and other approaches to keep a record of those capabilities. This is important, especially for companies whose main business lines depend on intangible aspects such as knowledge, innovation, service, prestige, and tradition. For technology-based organizations, knowing what its knowledge and innovation assets are, developing the appropriate intellectual property mechanisms, and creating value for them and for the society are of primary importance. By integrating BI, CI, and KM, SI gives an account of the main market trends, main competitors, new technologies and innovations, new products and services, research centers and intellectual capital formation, governmental policies and funding programs, venture capital, intellectual property regulations, and not-for-profit organizations, among the main business concerns. Thus, SI provides a company a way to meet the information needs of both its internal capabilities and those from the competitive environment.

This chapter is organized as follows: first, we describe the relevant background. Next we explain the SI methodology and the roadmap model for SI, and then we describe a Web and knowledge tool to support users in doing roadmap modeling. After this, we describe a case study for biological micro-electronic and mechanical systems (Bio-MEMS), and, finally, we present the conclusions of this study.

Background

BI, CI, and KM, and therefore SI, depend heavily on information and communication technologies (ICT). For instance, BI employs knowledge extraction and data-mining techniques borrowed from statistics, computer science, and artificial intelligence to learn useful patterns and knowledge hidden in large volumes of data that arise from business operations and transactions in an organization or that are stored in Web pages on the Internet (Anandarajan M., Anandarajan A., and Srinivasan, 2004). The same is true for CI in learning about its competitors from external sources and databases. BI/CI makes synergies with KM for capitalizing the knowledge assets of an organization for serving its clients in the best possible way to meet the company goals and increase the value of its stakeholders (Liebowitz, 1999, 2004). Data, text, and Web-mining techniques are used to drill into corporate databases and data warehouses for discovering knowledge that otherwise would be very difficult for a human to be aware of (Berry and Linoff, 2000). KM systems are implemented in an organization over the infrastructure provided by computer networks, telecommunications systems, electronic devices (PDAs, cell phones, etc.), database systems, digital libraries, and the Internet. Knowledge distribution and use among users worldwide are possible because of these technological advances (Aguirre, Brena, and Cantu, 2001).

MEMS arise from the integration of mechanical devices, electronic circuits, sensors, actuators, and other elements in a common silicon substratum through the technology of micromachining. The electronics side is based on CMOS integrated circuits (IC); the mechanical components are made using processes of micromachining that selectively records the tracks in the absent parts of the silicon capsule and adds new structural layers to form the mechanical and electromechanical devices. MEMS technologies have an ample rank of applications that include automobiles, telecommunications, aerospace, personal devices, global positioning systems, biochemistry, health, and medical equipment among the main areas. The Bio-MEMS field is understood as the application of MEMS technologies in biology, chemistry, environment, healthcare, and medicine. This industry has demonstrated its great potential in diverse areas of medicine and, most importantly, it contributes to improving the quality of life and health of humans. Both MEMS and Bio-MEMS are examples of emerging fields with a fast growth in the recent years. The Bio-MEMS industry is at an emerging stage of its development. The MEMSTAND Survey Analysis (Cui and Leach, 2003) reports that standards in a field are established when a technology is at a maturing stage, which is not the situation for MEMS, and, for this reason, standards are not found yet. Several roadmaps that integrate BI and KM concepts have been proposed and are being used in this field. These roadmaps present relevant information such as trends in market conditions, population growth, economics parameters, demand and mobility, legislative laws, and the growth of the global market in the use of these technologies. Nevertheless, these approaches are proprietary, are black boxes, and are not always supported by automated aids such as computer software or Web portals. In this research, we present an approach that comprises both a BI roadmap methodology as well as a Web-based portal for managing information and knowledge for Bio-MEMS technologies that serves users interested in this field.

SI is of great help in technology-oriented strategic domains such as MEMS-based industries. Technology roadmaps are the outcome of SI studies that serve users with information about technology trends and business opportunities. There are several roadmap approaches for MEMS, among which are the *NEXUS Microsystems Product-Technology Roadmap* (NEXUS, 2003), developed in Europe; the *Microsystems Research in Japan* (Howe et al., 2003), developed in the United States; and the *MANCEF Microsystems Top Down Nano Roadmap* (Elders and Walsh, 2002), developed in the United States (which has an international scope), among others.

In the following sections, we present an SI methodology that consists of roadmap model, a Web-knowledge-based tool for developing roadmaps, and a case study in the area of Bio-MEMS.

A Roadmap Model for SI

Roadmaps are standard tools in industries such as microelectronics, automotive, telecommunications, software, etc. In this section, we describe a roadmap model for guiding users in constructing roadmaps for prospective analysis and BI in a given industrial sector. The elements of the model are displayed in Figure 1.

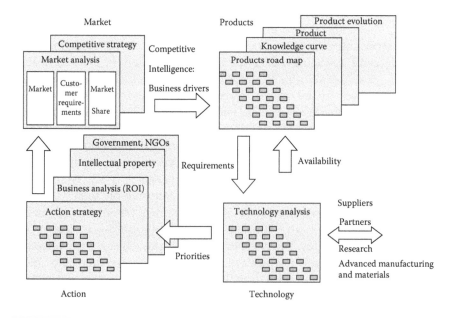

Figure 1   Roadmap model for SI.

The first step of the model is a market analysis to know who the competitors are, what the main products in the market and their characteristics are, what the market share of the competitors and their products is, what customer requirements are currently unmet by existing products, what the growth trends are, and similar measures. This step outputs a CI plan with business drivers and niche identification that are used in the next step. The second step is an analysis of the products that the company can deliver into the market based on its own competencies and capabilities. Data available on product performance, product evolution, and product benchmarking are analyzed to determine the competitive position of the company's products in the market and the niches identified. The result of this step is a set of requirements that are input to the third step on which a technology assessment is performed such that enhancements to products or research prototypes can be converted into actual products with innovations that should fill in niches and collocate the company in a better competitive position. Product design considers suppliers of parts and materials, partners, research prototypes from internal centers or research contract, advanced manufacturing technologies, and advanced materials from which the competitive advantage may come from to obtain a better product price or performance. Intellectual property issues such as patent filing are considered either to protect the company's technological developments, to prevent competitors from utilizing such innovations, or to enforce the technological image of the company. The result of this step is a set of priorities on new products and innovations that are input to the fourth step in which business actions are selected. Actions include a BI analysis with the calculation of return on investment (ROI) of the new products, the target market share, the impact of not-for-profit organizations such as nongovernmental agencies that may oppose or favor the new products, etc. The result of this fourth step is an action plan whose results are fed back into the first step to start a new cycle of the roadmap model.

Each of these four steps of the roadmap model deserves a full analysis of the elements and processes that conform them. In the following subsections, we present an overview of the main components of the model's steps.

Market Analysis

Market analysis is a CI study that provides answers to various questions among which are the following: who are the main competitors in the market and what are their main products; what are the main characteristics of those products; what is the market share of the competitors and their products; what customer requirements are currently unmet by existing products; what are the market growth trends; what is the maturity of the market, the products, and the technologies; what are the main macroeconomics factors about a block of countries or region of the world on which the company wants to compete; what are the main application domains prevalent in the market; and what the mergers and alliances taking place among competitors are. The answers to these and similar questions constitute a CI plan that includes business drivers and the identification of market niches on which the company may take a position. *Business drivers* are business opportunities identified during the analysis, such as new markets, product innovations, technologies, etc. For instance, the Internet was a fundamental driver for the development of many online, electronic businesses in most of the application domains. The DNA and the human genome project is an example of another driver for business development. Technological advances in nanotechnology, biotechnology, solar energy, space exploration, and other technologies contain important drivers for business development.

Products

Once business drivers and opportunities have been identified, an assessment of existing products and desirable innovations is performed as part of the roadmap model. The design for innovation is a key activity at this stage. This activity gathers data and information from customer satisfaction, competing products, new technologies, new markets, and other intelligence analysis elements. Competitive advantage may come in various forms; for instance, lowering product costs at the same time that functionality is increased. One example is found in the electronics industry in which cheaper and higher-capacity storage devices such as USBs, CDs, DVDs, and other storage devices are brought into the market each year. Another example is in the telecommunications industry, in which we find products such as cell phones, PDAs, laptops, and other communication devices with more functionality and lower prices. In the entertainment and music industry, innovative devices for video games and MP3 players appear in the market every year. Innovation in automobile design supported by technology results in cars models with improved security, functionality, and comfort each year. Other industries include home appliances, photography, medical equipment, industrial automation, etc.

Technology

As strategic industries are heavily technology dependent and oriented, R&D activities for the design and innovation of new product and services are essential for business growth. The type of research may be theoretical and basic; however, it is focused, problem driven, and motivated by the company's needs to remain competitive. Most multinational corporations invest five percent or more of their revenues in research and development either by funding their own R&D centers or by outsourcing them from R&D centers in universities or governmental laboratories and institutes. Many start-up companies are born based on ideas, prototypes, or patents invented by professors and students within research groups and laboratories in universities. The model gathers a comprehensive list of research and development centers in the field with information about their affiliations, lines of research, infrastructure, researchers, products, application domains, patents, morphological analysis of patents, licensing procedures, research expenditure, scientist education, rankings, and other related information.

Business Actions

Once the new product and services have been devised, business actions are selected. The roadmap model provides aids in investment scenario analysis and prospective ROI calculations on new products and services. The model also integrates information about economic blocks of countries with their R&D priorities, legislation characteristics, and other data such as national programs and expenditure, intellectual property regulations, foreign investment policies, cooperation agreements, international rankings, level of population education, labor capacities, national resources, labor union policies, and other related issues that become important for business decisions. The roadmap model considers relevant aspects of intellectual property such as statistics about patents per county, economic block, company, pirating practices and piracy protection, international treaties, and intellectual protection agencies. The model also gathers information about potential angel investors and venture capitals for technology licensing and creation of spin-off companies. A search is done of all the available sources for building a database of investors. Professional, scientific, and nongovernmental organizations are considered by the roadmap model as they may influence aspects of an industrial market. Examples are human rights, environment protection, democracy, standardization associations, the United Nations, etc.

Roadmap Modeling Results

The roadmap modeling yields outcomes and drivers for each of the four steps, such as reports with information about market trends, patterns, indicators, rankings, correlations, graphs, distributions, statistics, listings, benchmarks, and other useful information for decision analysis. The following section describes the automation facilities of a Web tool associated to the roadmap model.

A Knowledge-Based Tool for SI

We describe a Web tool that is part of the knowledge-based entrepreneurial portal described in Cantu et al. (2005a). The tool is a computer framework that helps users in conducting SI studies by supporting and complementing the roadmap model with automated analysis facilities for data acquisition, storage, organization, and knowledge extraction and distribution. Data is acquired from information sources that include hard-copy materials, Web home pages, and electronic files such as databases, data warehouses, and digital libraries with text, images, and videos. Some databases and hard-copy materials are proprietary and must be bought. Some databases and printed materials are public domain, but they must be searched. The purpose of the data extraction process is to help users in finding the roadmap outcomes and drivers. This extraction process is supported by a set of data mining, text mining, and morphological analysis tools, as illustrated in Figure 2.

Some of the information sources are hard-copy printed materials such as books, manuals, journals, magazines, status reports, or proprietary roadmaps that must be bought from publishers or professional associations. Automating search in these materials is more difficult, and an analyst who reads and extracts the relevant material from these sources is needed. Alternatively, provided copyrights are preserved, these materials may be digitized with permission from the authors and publishers. In any case, the outcome goes to a digital storage in a word-processing document, spreadsheet, or database.

A great deal of information, both public domain and proprietary, is found in Web pages. This information is about companies, products, foundations, associations, etc. Reports, trends, and benchmarks are found this way. Electronic files such as databases, document repositories, software tools, and other sources are found on the Internet. Some are proprietary, and some are public domain.

Source information is organized in the Web tool through a digital library and internal databases. The Phronesis digital library was used for storing, searching, and exchanging electronic documents. The databases were implemented in the open source MySQL database server that offers multistorage engine architecture, flexibility, database management system, speed, compactness, stability, and cross-platform support. The URL is available upon request.

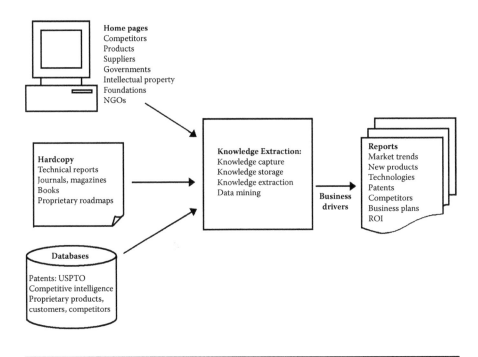

Figure 2   Knowledge extraction using the knowledge-based tool.

Knowledge Extraction and Data Analysis Techniques

Knowledge extraction facilities are an important element of a Web tool. The extraction is supported by data-mining, pattern recognition, and statistical analysis techniques. Data-mining techniques include decision tree learning that uses the entropy, GINI index, and CHAID rules. Pattern recognition techniques cover neural network and Bayesian network learning. Among the statistical analysis tools, we find filtering and classification such as averaging, regression, correlation, clustering, analysis of variance, and hypotheses testing. By combining various techniques, we construct the roadmap outputs.

The current implementation of the knowledge extraction is done offline using a data-mining environment developed by the authors and their students (Cantu et al., 2005b). The Web tool generates electronic files that are converted into data-mining tables for knowledge extraction. Document data analysis is carried out through the search engine implemented in the Phronesis digital library. Currently, a URL search on the Web is done by using public-domain search engines. The Web tool architecture is depicted in Figure 3.

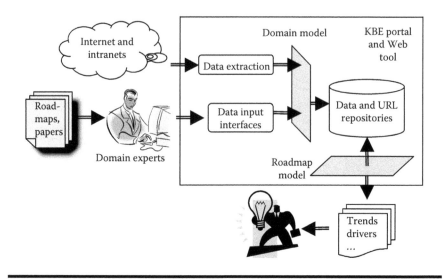

Figure 3   Web tool architecture.

The Bio-MEMS Case Study

The roadmap model is now illustrated with the Bio-MEMS case study (Cantu et al., 2005a). We describe the roadmap model following the steps shown in Figure 1. The roadmap model proved useful in organizing and extracting the relevant information for this industry by way of its automation facilities. We describe the roadmap model steps to analyze the Bio-MEMS sector and explain the main findings, results, and recommendations. In this chapter, we present an overview of the four steps of the roadmap model. A thorough description can be found in Mora et al., 2004.

The Bio-MEMS roadmap model contains a worldwide market survey of 180 companies, including areas of application, market share, new materials, fabrication processes, and standards; the main products in the market; the technologies developed at a group of 113 research centers and programs in Bio-MEMS; and sensible business actions for company development. The model also contains the programs pushed by the governments of the United States, Japan, and European countries such as England, Germany, France, etc., and the situation of the industry in these countries; the statistics of 100 patents and intellectual property consideration in countries, companies, application areas, and products; and information about investors, and the main not-for-profit organizations, including standardization agencies and scientific associations.

For the market analysis step, the roadmap model includes Bio-MEMS market trends, the main companies, and application domains. Other issues include fabrication materials and suppliers, manufacturing processes, and standardization.

Bio-MEMS Market Trends

The Bio-MEMS industry has advanced quickly, and new products have been manufactured. Medical equipment manufacturing is already using this technology. This is because of its numerous advantages such as reduced size, low costs of mass production of devices in the same substratum, the great diversity of materials used, and the high functionality and reliability that they present. However, there still are obstacles such as the very strict governmental regulations in the medical field, the extensive proofs, high R&D costs, and lack of standards. The MEMSTAND Survey analysis has predicted that in 2007 and 2008, the first standardization will be adopted. The Bio-MEMS tendency of growth predicted a market of $4 billion for 2004 and represented 40 percent of the total MEMS market in 2003.

Bio-MEMS Companies

The search for Bio-MEMS companies resulted in a list of 180 companies active in the field. The 180 companies were selected from the three most important economics blocks: the United States, Asia Pacific, and the European community. These companies were identified by reading specialized journals, business newspapers, MEMS roadmaps and consulting reports, and commercial databases. The companies were selected by a specialized group and were fed into our databases. Their country distribution is summarized in Table 1.

Bio-MEMS Application Domains

The main Bio-MEMS application domains were identified to analyze general trends. The domains were used in the classification of Bio-MEMS products, companies, and universities. Clustering statistical techniques were used for this purpose. The application domains are the following:

- *Diagnostic/analysis:* This domain includes biochemical analyses and biological tests in fluids/aerosols, drug detection, and diseases.
- *Monitoring:* This domain is about detecting biological signals. Products include glucose, pressure, blood, and gas sensors.
- *Bioactuators and implants:* Bioactuators are used to reproduce mechanical actions through micropumps and microvalves. Products include implants for ear prosthetics and artificial retinas.

Table 1 Number of Bio-MEMS Companies per Country	
Country	*Bio-MEMS Companies*
United States	66
Japan	28
United Kingdom	15
France	5
Germany	21
Switzerland	6
Sweden	8
China	3
Denmark	10
Others	18
Total	180

Table 2 Industry Trends per Application	
Application Area	*Bio-MEMS Companies*
Diagnosis and analysis	44
Biosensors	85
Instrumentation and equipment	31
Bioactuators and implants	46

- *Medical instrumentation:* This domain is about medical equipment and surgical instrumentation. Products include microneedles, microcameras, and microrobots.
- *MEMS environmental technology:* This domain is about pollution, water, and gas analysis. Products include electronic noses for air pollution control.

Company statistics per application domain are illustrated in Table 2. MEMS applications for medical instrumentation and diagnosis/analysis include the following (NEXUS, 2003):

- Endoscope to extract cell and swab to withdraw cells at different areas of the human body
- Exhaler air sensors

- Internal ultrasonic sensors, esophagus inspection camera, blood withdrawal needle
- Body fluids analysis equipment: needle, coating, urine

MEMS application for implants and actuators includes the following (NEXUS, 2003):

- Eye, shoulder, cochlear, dropped foot implants
- Heart pacemakers
- Pumping of lung air, blood, and other body liquids
- Control system for nerve motion detection and stimulation

For the product analysis step, the roadmap model describes the main Bio-MEMS products in the market and its own products. Other issues include fabrication materials and suppliers, manufacturing processes, and standardization.

Bio-MEMS Products

Biochips are considered a killer application. They are used in detecting infectious diseases such as HIV, DNA analysis, proteins, and genotypes. A market of $3 billion for biochips was foretold for 2004. Predictions included a growth of 800 percent for DNA chips and 1000 percent for protein chips. Figure 4 shows growth trends by product. Another market

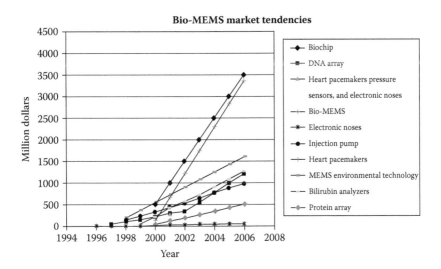

Figure 4   Bio-MEMS products trends.

is the environmental-technology-based in MEMS used for polluting-particle detection, explosives and drug detection, and water analysis using electronic noses, with sales in 1998 of $200 million and $900 million in 2002.

Bio-MEMS Materials

The materials' own mechanical, optical, electrical, or chemical properties are used depending on the application. MEMS in biological and medical applications use materials different from silicon. Bio-MEMS materials such as carbon, polymers, polyamides, EAP (electroactive polymer), metal, ceramic, quartz, glass, and SU-8 are commonly used.

Bio-MEMS Manufacturing and Packaging

This depends on the type of application and materials used. Manufacturing technologies comprise assembling, packaging, and testing. Bio-MEMS that use standard packaging are those that still use silicon materials, such as pressure sensors, microvalves, micropumps, etc. Some of them had adopted standard packaging techniques with bulk and surface micromachining or photolithography. Other packaging techniques are flip-chip and single-chip integration, commonly used in humidity and *in vivo* sensors. Commercial sensors that use SOI are electronic noses, ultrasonic gas sensors, DNA chips, and pacemakers. Regarding manufacturing, Bio-MEMS with a great variety of materials use LIGA (lithographic galvanoformung abformung) micromachining in commercial products such as micropumps, microreactors, microspectrometers, bilirubin analyzers, and microengines. LIGA microengines are used successful by the European chemical industry and IMM, Mainz, Germany. Companies involved in Bio-MEMS commercial products, packaging techniques, manufacturing technology include Motorola, Biotronik, Nanogem, Genum, etc.

Bio-MEMS Standardization

There are no MEMS standards yet in manufacturing processes, materials, and terminology. Surveys consider that Bio-MEMS materials, size, and forms will be the first standards in 2007 or 2008 (Cui and Leach, 2003). Regarding materials standardization, substrates different from those used in semiconductors are considered. Packaging and biocompatibility are becoming standards in testing and optical measuring under mechanical and chemical conditions.

Table 3 R&D Centers by Economic Blocks and Application Domain

	Diagnosis and Analysis	Biosensors	Implants	Environmental
United States	19	11	6	0
Europe	16	17	6	4
Asia Pacific	23	13	11	1

For the **technology** analysis step, the roadmap model describes the main Bio-MEMS R&D centers, government programs, and intellectual property.

R&D Centers

Statistics about R&D centers in Bio-MEMS R&D were considered for the three most important commercial blocks, Asia Pacific, Europe, and the United States, to analyze the Bio-MEMS research tendencies. Asia Pacific was the strongest in R&D in Bio-MEMS implants and diagnostic/analysis, and Europe in monitoring and MEMS technological environment as shown in Table 3.

Governments: Bio-MEMS Investments and Programs

Research and infrastructure expenditure by governments in MEMS were also identified. Examples include the following: In Korea, nanotechnology, biotechnology, and information systems are considered the three highest priorities. In China, microsensors and Bio–MEMS are also high priorities with an emphasis in MEMS manufacturing and nanotechnology. In Israel, energy and water are high priorities followed by telecommunications, nanotechnology, biotechnology, and software. Also, R&D in universities is concentrated in chemistry and materials. In Japan, high-priority programs supported by governmental funds and priorities are biotechnology, analytical chemistry, energy systems, and microgeneration. Industry and university interaction is increasing through specific MEMS programs and new university study programs based on MEMS (Howe et al., 2003).

Regarding *investors* in Bio-MEMS, the KBE roadmap found information about potential investors in countries such as Germany, Korea, and the United States for a total of approximately $7 billion (Mora et al., 2004).

Intellectual Property Organizations: Bio-MEMS Patents, Trends, and Reports

Patent analysis in Bio-MEMS was carried out by searching for patents in various intellectual property databases, such as Banco Nacional de Patentes del IMPI (BANAPANET), United States Patent and Trademark Office (USPTO), European Patent Office (ESPACENET), etc. The KBE study selected 100 patents in medical areas such as oncology, diabetes, ophthalmology, genetic, and clinical analyses.

The KBE roadmap searched through the 180 Bio-MEMS companies to know their patents and applications. The roadmap identified patents issued in Mexico obtaining Bio-MEMS company reports by patents and medicals areas. Considering BANAPANET, USPTO, and ESPACENET, Figure 5 shows the R&D Bio-MEMS tendency with respect to patents per country using USPTO.

For the **business action** step, a business action plan is generated with information about the introduction of new or improved products into the market, the calculation of the ROI of those products and its business plan, and an assessment of risks coming from governmental policies, intellectual property regulations in target countries, and potential investors. The roadmap model gathered information about 50 nonprofit Bio-MEMS organizations that have invested in Bio-MEMS R&D (Mora et al., 2004).

Tool Support for the Bio-MEMS Case Study

The Bio-MEMS roadmap was obtained with the support of the Sistema de Inteligencia Tecnologico Empresarial en MEMS (SITE-MEMS), which is the name of the Web, knowledge-based tool for the MEMS application domain. SITE-MEMS was implemented in a Web environment using Hypertext Preprocessor (PHP), Java Server Pages (JSP), PHP-Collab, Phronesis, and other proprietary programming systems. The user interaction, navigation, and manual data input are scripted in PHP, which is a widely used general-purpose scripting language, is specially suited for Web development, and can be embedded into HTML. PHP-Collab is an open source Internet-enabled collaboration workspace for project teams. PHP-Collab architecture allows the consulting team to share information in one space and publish that information when desired to another space for the client. In addition, it encompasses the most important aspects of project management, such as task planning and document sharing, and hooks into other open source applications for bug tracking, content management, and ongoing project support. The SITE-MEMS provides a Web user interface shown in Figure 6. It shows the user option for user collaboration, roadmap modeling, knowledge extraction and data analysis, search, and Web links.

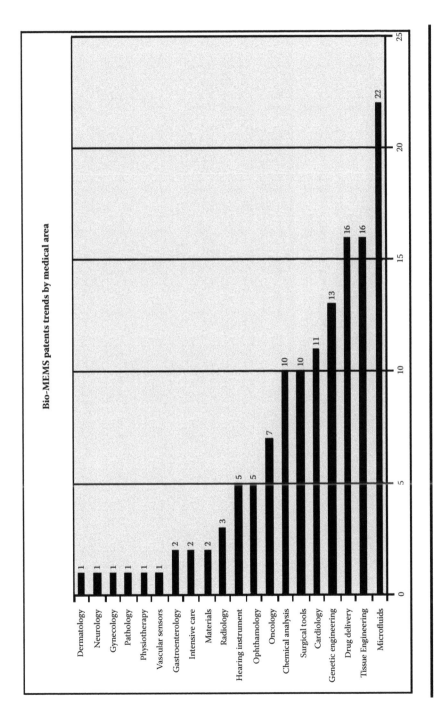

Figure 5 Bio-MEMS patent trends in medicine.

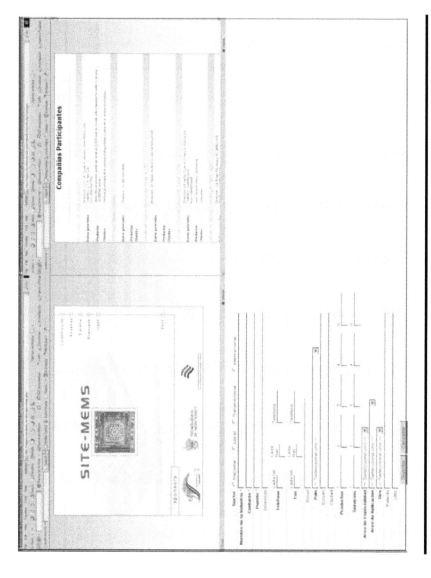

Figure 6   SITE-MEMS user interface.

Conclusions

We presented a methodology for SI in technology-based businesses at industrial sectors. The methodology was used for advising users regarding business decisions. It includes both a roadmap model as well as a knowledge-based tool applicable to various technologies and industries. The methodology is supported by automated aids such as a Web portal and data-mining package with facilities to update data and knowledge bases in a continuous way. This is the dynamic feature of the approach. The second feature is transportability, which means that the roadmap and knowledge-based tool are applicable to various domains. We used the Bio-MEMS case to illustrate the methodology with a survey of 180 companies, 113 research centers, and around 100 patents. The roadmap model provided information about the market, the main products, the technology, and the business actions. The tool uses automation facilities such as digital libraries, searching and knowledge extraction from databases, data warehouses, and the Web. These features facilitate roadmap construction. The functionality of the tool will be improved with ROI calculations, scenario analysis and more statistics, and machine learning techniques that will operate in an online environment.

Acknowledgment

This research was sponsored by the United States–Mexico Foundation for Science (FUMEC), the Ministry of Economy in Mexico, and the Instituto Tecnológico y de Estudios Superiores de Monterrey. We thank Guillermo Fernandez de la Garza, FUMEC's general director for suggesting this project and for his valuable guidelines during the development of the project.

References

Aguirre, J.L., Brena, R., and Cantu, F.J., Multiagent-based knowledge networks, *Expert Systems with Applications: An International Journal*, No. 20, 65–75, 2001.

Ajzen, I., The theory of planned behavior, *Organizational Behavior and Human Decision Processes*, Vol. 50, No. 2, 179–211, 1991.

Anandarajan, M., Anandarajan, A., and Srinivasan, C., *Business Intelligence Techniques*, Springer-Verlag, Heidelberg, 2004.

Berry, M. and Linoff, G., *Mastering Data Mining: The Art and Science of Customer Relationship Management*, John Wiley & Sons, New York, 1997.

Cantu, F.J., Mora, S.P., Diaz, J.A., Ceballos, H.G., Martinez, S.O., and Jimenez, D.R., A knowledge-based entrepreneurial approach for business intelligence in strategic technologies: Bio-MEMS, *Proceedings of the 11th Americas Conference on Information Systems*, Omaha, NE, August 11–14, 2005a.

Cantu, F.J., Ceballos, H., Mora, S.P., and Escoffie, M.A., A Knowledge-based information system for managing research programs and value creation in a university environment, *Proceedings of the 11th Americas Conference on Information Systems*, Omaha, NE, August 11–14, 2005b.

Cui, Z. and Leach, R., The industry and market for Microsystems technology, *MEMSTAND Standardization Roadmap*, 8, 9, 2003.

Elders, J. and Walsh, S., *International MEMS, Microsystems, Top Down Nano Roadmap*, ISBN: 0-9727333-0-2; MANCEF, Naples, FL, 2002.

Howe, R.T., Allen, M.G., Berlin, A.A., Hui, E.E., Monk, D.J., Najafi, K., and Yamakawa, M., WTEC Panel on Microsystems Research in Japan, Final report, sponsored by the National Science Foundation (NSF) and other agencies of the U.S. government, 2003.

Liebowitz, J., *Addressing the Human Capital Crisis in the Federal Government: A Knowledge Management Perspective*, Elsevier/Butterworth-Heinemann, Burlington, MA, 2004.

Liebowitz, J. (Ed.), *Knowledge Management Handbook*, CRC Press, Boca Raton, FL, 1999.

NEXUS, *The Nexus Product-Technology Roadmap for Microsystems*, ISBN 2-9518607-1-4, The NEXUS Association, Grenoble, France, September 2003.

Mora, S.P., Diaz A., Hernandez A., Alejandra, R., Daniel, J., and Sergio, M. (2004), Mapa Tecnológico — Micro Sistemas Electro Mecánicos Biológicos — BioMEMS, sponsored by Ministry of Economic, and the United States-Mexico Foundation for Science, Abril, Monterrey, Mexico.

Salinas, F.A. and Garza S.D. (2004), Arquitectura de Múltiples Capas y Orientada a Servicios para el Sistema Phronesis, Master Science thesis in computer science technology, ITESM Press, México.

Vitt, E., Luckevich, M., and Misner, S., *Business Intelligence Making Better Decisions Faster*, Microsoft Press, WA, 2002.

Semiconductor CI — From Current Awareness to Predictive Decision Making: Building a Best-of-Breed CI Program at a Top-Tier Global IC Manufacturer

Arik Johnson

Introduction

Every moderately successful enterprise in history — business or otherwise — has used competitive intelligence (CI) to manifest a mission of serving its customers' needs better than alternatives or their functional equivalents. This is a truth that defies the differences of degree that describe the depth and breadth of CI functions in business today. Indeed, most CI activities are exceedingly informal and "tactical" in nature, focused on the inexorable penetration of existing markets through the retention and capture of customers and market share away from zero-sum, direct rivals using incremental innovations to existing product lines as the basis of buying and selling decisions. Even among this rich, though myopic, universe of current-awareness-driven CI practices, there is very rarely concern directed toward more predictive capabilities of "strategic" CI or its ability to assist executive decision making, despite its increasing importance in an era in which regulators and shareholders alike demand greater reliability of forecasted earnings. Financial results are to be based on fact, not fiction, and risks to the forecast could serve as grounds to charges of criminal misconduct.

The fact is, it is an elusive truth that existing competitors, risks, and other threats to the status quo rarely have game-changing impacts on any business. It is more often a factor of consumer trends, technology changes, and political, social, or environmental factors that converge to influence market demand away from one source of value and toward another.

Only CI can furnish the outward-looking perspective required to master such predictive capabilities, both to assist the firm in becoming operationally more efficient in its current lines of business (LOBs) while simultaneously becoming more strategically effective when selecting markets in which to invest and compete.

Over the summer of 1999, I met a woman at a CI summit in San Diego who was on assignment from a Fortune 500 global semiconductor manufacturer headquartered in the United States. She came seeking advice from experts and colleagues on how to deploy a CI program at her firm, after recently having taken charge of the task on orders from her company's executive management team (EMT).

We met during my preconference workshop on that very subject — although it was less of a workshop than a round-table-style interactive dialog that I facilitated between CI operational peers, designed to share best practices among participants. The following day, after a shorter, one-hour presentation during general session, she approached me about assisting on a consulting basis to help enable their plan.

This is the story of that firm and how they used CI to build competitive awareness and predictability. In the end, it became a more effective decision-making enterprise at all levels, still making the hard choices about structure and strategy required of every successful business venture to a sustain competitive advantage in existing markets in the nearer term.

Though you would instantly recognize the name if I told you, I use this necessarily anonymous example to illustrate what I have learned from my own peers to be the prototypical experience of CI advisors everywhere — that is, the circumstances under which a new consulting and support client turns to specialists such as ourselves for advice, the drivers of this approach, and the risks and benefits to be addressed in doing so. For CI experts, many of the anecdotes and vignettes will be familiar, and you are likely to find yourself nodding along. Still, every CI deployment story is unique, and this discussion will hopefully furnish an opportunity for readers of all kinds to begin to see some of the probable challenges and opportunities they will face as they seek to learn more about CI best practices.

Backstory: The Element of Surprise

The week after the conference I traveled to her site and met the team she had assembled to execute the plan, as it then existed, to deploy their CI program.

An interdisciplinary team consisting of a representative of the corporate library, an IT staffer who shared 50 percent of her time, two research analysts drawn from the market research team, a college intern (there for the remainder of the summer, eventually offered a full-time position in the group), and my primary contact from the conference, the woman with the primary task of program director and "evangelist." Her job was to simultaneously construct the infrastructure and processes to enable the CI process and roll out the system to the enterprise for immediate needs. Likewise, she needed to develop a business plan and strategy for the evolution and development of the CI program while also deciding which internal constituents to aim both her sales and marketing messaging to, then which of those eventual customers to prioritize, and when to go after them. This was an afterthought, and virtually my first recommendation was to avoid the chronic "flash-in-the-pan" syndrome — that is, a costly and protracted build-up followed by a short and troubled life cycle, ending in a spectacular flame-out before being dismantled and having its staff reassigned.

When I asked my cornerstone contextual question of what had ignited such urgency for this new initiative, she replied — as so many often do with some variation on circumstances — that a low-cost competitor from Asia had recently surprised them by acquiring a majority interest in a common tier-one vendor of theirs. This competitor would, from now on, make fulfillment of product manufacturing exceedingly more difficult in two of their five primary lines of business (LOBs) (representing greater than 50 percent of revenues).

This would ultimately force the company to look elsewhere for the essential component inputs required at a significant increase in the firm's cost of production, with the eventual "sun-setting" of the marketability of those products as competitive dynamics dictated market evolution back toward new competitive equilibrium. This strategic surprise had introduced a factor of "structural risk" that should at best have been avoided or at least planned for. In addition, the EMT was taking this opportunity to deploy the multifaceted CI program that they had always wanted, resulting in a mandate governed by committee and, therefore, lacking a concrete point of first attack.

Instead of forging a spear, she had been told to fashion an axe.

Based on her background in "industry analyst relations," the company's management team had called her in to a meeting between leaders from around the firm to address the situation and why they could not have seen this game-changing surprise coming. After all, with the benefit of hindsight, it seemed obvious to them that such a move was at least possible, even probable and, at worst, predictable. How could they have been so blind as to fail having seen this coming? Why didn't they preempt the deal themselves? They vowed never to be surprised again and decided on a chain-of-command that made CI a new function, reporting to world-wide sales and marketing.

Similar to many members of the global "ecology" associated with the making of integrated circuits (IC), her firm was a member of an industry trade group, and she was its primary liaison. This role afforded the company greater predictability in intra-industry relations to help forecast supply and demand so that no shortage or glut of products would diminish the value of such multibillion-dollar investments as constructing new wafer fabrication plants and other such costly expenditures. Thereby, this new risk in the international marketplace would be lessened.

In this largely outward-facing role, she was also the chief liaison of the company's analyst relations program, which interfaced directly with both Wall Street financial analysts as well as the external market research houses that forecast market dynamics as part of her parent investor relations team, with a dual reporting hierarchy as part of the PR function of the marketing department. It seemed a natural fit for a woman of her perspective to also head up the CI function, a practice that was little used at the time but has since become a much more commonplace approach, particularly among semiconductor manufacturers.

Finally, I learned that, over the previous 20 years, such surprises seemed to occur with some regularity and coincided immediately thereafter with the company's redeployment of something analogous to a CI program precisely to avoid such surprises in the future. In fact, there had been no fewer than three previous such initiatives in the prior decade, punctuating the high-risk, high-reward nature of such a role. And, because failure would be met with the swift and sure scrubbing of the program, followed shortly by a wholesale realignment of resources to try again later, these circumstances were, in fact, predictable.

The context described so far would seem to be anomalous to CI "best practices." However, I have ironically found this situation to be relatively commonplace, especially among large companies, often pivoting on the fleeting whims of such impermanent affairs as staffing assignments or a swing in the business cycle. My own anecdotal observations point to the CI group most often looked on as overhead to be "right-sized" out of existence whenever cuts are required to maintain the bottom line, particularly when its structure revolves around a centralized department with subordinately remote hierarchical influence in the lines of real strategic decision making. It is only those CI groups that can transcend what is really more a problem of image and evangelism that create true sustainability and go on to earn the respect and loyalty of the myriad customer groups that might come to rely on their advice and recommendations.

We have come to describe this much more entrepreneurial approach to creating value from CI on a sustainable basis as, in effect, incorporating a business-within-a-business philosophy of serving customers and delivering CI products and services to those customers in unique and differentiated ways from functionally equivalent alternatives. Incidentally, the substitute for this entrepreneurial approach has usually been manifold in its service to far less integrated attempts at fortifying and proving the existential value of the CI function based on its empirical indispensability. That is, let us focus on using more sophisticated analytical tools, models, and frameworks (thereby highlighting the analytical intellect of the team), while attempting to quantify virtually impossible-to-measure return-on-investment metrics (thereby highlighting the bottom-line dollars-and-cents contribution of the team). A holistic approach to ROI is required that leverages all of these factors, but the end goal should be on serving core customers first and best.

The easiest way to strengthen this existential argument is to instead concentrate on providing customers with quick wins to earn their confidence and trust and to always prioritize customers based on their identity to the CI team's core mission. It is not that you will serve lesser masters any less; it is simply an attitude that some customers are more important to CI's functional sustainability than others and, when resource allocations require prioritization, as they eventually will, it is understood where the sacrifices are to be made. With this in mind, the CI staff can charge forward and become a sort of internal consulting group to clients, a real-time and on-demand think tank who can examine the options available and recommend the actions that will be required to build advantage for the company.

At its highest level, the CI function becomes a true trusted advisor and can be described most concisely as representing by proxy the organization's external market forces and their reactive dynamics to various actions under consideration for the firm — in essence, filling the shoes and representing the perspective and resultant actions of customers, competitors, vendors and even investors, regulators, and other actors. This sort of intuition about behavior from the external marketplace is rare and necessary to effective decision support.

Where to Begin: Benchmarking Comparative Practices

With this in mind, we set about the foundational business plan development required to validate the provisioning of start-up resources — from budget and headcount to charter, mission, and values, as well as process mapping to determine infrastructure requirements expected for year one, with projected modifiers out through year five.

The first step involved benchmarking comparative CI programs to capture the lessons learned from these other firms — most significantly in terms of ongoing outcomes, creating best practice alliances with similarly sized, noncompeting organizations from outside the semiconductor industry supplemented by short, ad hoc studies of direct, tier-one competitors to create a baseline recommendation for rollout. This was the basis of argument for resource allocation changes in headcount, time frame, and budget.

Industry peers at first appeared to suffer from similar dynamics with regard to the circumstances involved in establishing their own internal CI departments, with the exception of one particularly long-lived and high-impact team at a firm in the consumer electronics industry. Using these benchmarking lessons to extract the patterns for success and failure from this sample particular to this type of firm, as well as those best-of-breed firms with similar industry dynamics but who excelled extraordinarily, we structured a hybrid of tactical and strategic CI objectives and service priorities for year one, with a gradual implementation time frame to be completed by year five, if all went according to plan.

We did this knowing, of course, that keeping to plan was somewhat less than realistic, finding to our great surprise a marked acceleration of the program as described in the following text, ultimately arriving at our aggregate goals by the end of year two, almost three years ahead of schedule.

The explanation is complex. First, because of the benchmarking activity at the beginning, executive management erred on the side of overfunding the program and providing a less intense implementation schedule to attack high-priority objectives. This furnished the chance to really work with internal clients one-on-one to determine their needs and decide on a relationship structure customized to their circumstances, but which also would scale to new target clientele. The patience and generosity of oversight in this example is atypical, but was the predominant factor in the program's smooth implementation.

A Hybridized Model and Gradual Implementation

Because we had to serve simultaneously the five LOBs by satisfying their mostly tactical CI needs, as well as the corporate executive management team with its more forward-looking strategic perspective focused on early warning and emerging threat assessment, it was decided a hybrid model of centralized collection and analysis with a more gradual implementation schedule determined by completing implementation with each of the target clients would work to our advantage and allow us to accelerate completion of each phase as opportunity permits while fortifying customer relationships in the process.

The most frequent portfolio of tactical CI products and services equipped the LOBs with the ability to become more efficient and agile in predicting customer needs in the marketplace even while they were occupied with competing day-to-day for new business.

The following LOB-directed CI support services crossed a diverse set of CI output categories, mostly directed at sales, marketing and product management, and development topics:

- Prospect win/loss analysis
- Prospect RFP deal-support design and prototype
- Customer product roadmapping
- Customer "wallet share" and "low-hanging fruit"
- Competitor sell-against strategy
- Competitor input sample acquisition (tear-down and reverse engineering)
- Value-chain monitoring (competitors and vendors) on price, products, performance, and positioning
- Operational and performance benchmarking on inventory turnover, sales force structure, and cost of production
- Market profiling of competitive posture, functional equivalency, customer trends, key-player profiles, five-year total available market (TAM), and compound annual growth rate (CAGR) projects

In addition to these mostly tactical issues, the EMT was chiefly concerned with being in the right businesses to grow those businesses quickly that represented the greatest route to aggregate growth for the company. They were also interested in potentially divesting those assets that did not match the firm's core competency. EMT leadership had a short list of very focused top-tier strategic issues:

- Positioning (invest/divest) across the value chain to match long-term consumption trends
- Intellectual property and access to strategic technologies for product differentiation
- Mergers, acquisitions, and alliance opportunities
- Expansion planning across LOBs

Finally, while engaging in each of these diverse support activities for the two primary constituencies, the CI program was engaged with other internal partners, primarily in corporate management offices:

- Trade show and conference intelligence with marketing
- Creating a culture of competitive intelligence with human resources
- Counter-intelligence awareness building with security
- Automating CI's discovery and dissemination architecture with IT

Operationally, this approach provided liaison between CI and a diverse collection of multidisciplinary customers and collaborators that needed to be served through a common user interface — an entry page to a PDF database on the company's intranet — while also furnishing the ability to engage ad hoc projects that could scale well to meet fast-changing needs by new customers.

In this respect, regardless of the particular partner or set of partners a CI director chooses to select for such commissioned and ad hoc fulfillment, it should be said that no CI program can be expected to scale to meet new customer needs without a qualified, knowledgeable external partner to subcontract and outsource part or all of the collection and analysis work to. My firm, Aurora, actually recommended several others with specialized expertise in particular collection and analysis techniques, industries, markets, and environments with which to work. In the end, of an annual budget of approximately $2 million at the time, nearly half of that went outside to hire external fulfillment support of episodic client needs, or it was budgeted for subscriptions to periodic information services more efficiently produced outside.

The outcomes of the relationship with just one of the LOBs this first year, one of those most in need of its help, the CI team worked with the "Communications" products group to:

- Capture new share of two major customers, Motorola and Nokia, with mixed-signal design wins for next-generation 3G mobile handsets
- Conduct the first of what became a regular trade show collection and analysis "war-room" at the COMDEX trade show in Las Vegas
- Predict (and helped avert) the last-minute loss of a cornerstone design-win to a "fab-less" start-up firm competing for the Bluetooth radio in Compaq's second-generation iPAQ handheld
- Influence the purchase of an IP-only engineering firm active in the deployment of automotive telematics products
- Deliver a 15-min intranet-based counter-intelligence awareness training presentation, in partnership with the security department, to alert personnel throughout the company to the possibility of CI conducted against them
- Deploy a newsfeed programmed with a taxonomy that covered every one of the company's major customer and product groups (earlier delivered via daily e-mail update)
- Integrate the newsfeed in XML with a new "weblogging" application that allowed for impact analysis, implications, further due diligence, and collaborative recommendations development for those clients affected
- Learn the cost of production to within five percent of the actual cost for 30 categories of wafers manufactured by a top competitor
- Discover that dynamic pricing techniques were required to accelerate inventory turns of a lagging product family for reducing latent inventory life cycles
- Compare and recommend changes in organization to the company's international sales force designed to structure the firm to better satisfy customer needs
- Help to identify a buyer for a promising but tragically underperforming product family that ultimately went on to dominate its market in the hands of that more appropriate owner
- Build and promote a "hotline" for capturing rumors among staff about competitively relevant activities in the external marketplace
- Advise the sales force on developing a comprehensive yet simple sell-against strategy for how to compete with particular competitors, depending on which situations called for particular comparisons
- Learn that a major cable set-top box customer was buying a majority of signal processing silicon from a competitor with inferior technology and advise sales force on sales factors affecting selection

Year Two: Consolidation and Building the Knowledge-Base Taxonomy

With a diverse portfolio of first-year wins behind them, the CI team set about indexing their findings to a content management system within their small server on the intranet. ROI metrics were established based primarily on customer satisfaction, escaping more empirical measurements, but not abandoning them altogether. It is, of course, still desirable to understand how much a customer is worth to the company and how much is put at risk in their defection.

After brainstorming structure and user interface, they created a three-dimensional matrix of classifiers that could map well to the three dimensions of KITs, or Key Intelligence Topics. These dimensions began with the x-axis of key players (customers, competitors, vendors, etc.), expanding to the y-axis the five LOB categories and three geographies (due to their global footprint and divisional structure across Americas, EMEA, and Asia Pacific, with a total of 15 categories), and the z-axis of activities and behaviors, which includes everything from new product development to management personnel changes.

This approach to categorization of the taxonomy for what became a true knowledge base was later supplanted by enterprise search software that built "dynamic taxonomies" simply by indexing what was present in structured and unstructured data sources and then displaying a taxonomy on the basis of the topics contained therein. Though expensive, this approach offered incredible efficiencies in manpower and greater accuracy in the analysis of intersections among the three dimensions. This has created a platform to push CI products to internal customers, while they can pull services and pay for them from their own budgets, resulting in a stable budget year-to-year for the program.

As of this writing in mid-2005, this is today leading to what can only be called *truly predictive analytics* — the ability to see patterns emerging in this knowledge base, and then hypothesizing on likely outcomes from these patterns. This is, without a doubt, an imperfect science, but one that the management sincerely hopes can offer the benefits of 20/20 hindsight without the painful lessons only otherwise offered by experience.

INDEX

Index